Visions
ALONG THE
Poudre
Valley

For Alan

BY

Enjoy!

PHIL WALKER

Phil Walker 10/7/95

Visions Along The Poudre Valley

Library of Congress Catalog Card Number 95-92475

ISBN 1-887982-00-0

Produced by The Old Army Press, Fort Collins, CO
Printed in the United States of America by Citizen Printing Company

Published by
Philip Walker Communications
To order books or audio cassettes contact:
Walker Communications
636 Cheyenne Dr. #11
Fort Collins, CO 80525

Dedication

To
The People of Fort Collins.
For all you have been, and for all
you are yet to become.

Acknowledgements

Visions Along the Poudre Valley is a presentation
to Fort Collins through the community citizenship
and gracious support of:
The Everitt Companies, especially Bob Everitt
First State Bank, Tom Byington, President
Coldwell-Banker, Everitt/Williams Real Estate
Foothills Fashion Mall

. . . technical support:
Advertising Development Specialists
Rick Roesener, Project Coordinator
Linda Roesener, Manuscript Editor
Denise Znamenacek-Knuppel, Graphic Design
Two Eagles Communications:
The "Eagle" 96.1 FM
The "Bear" 107.9 FM
Z-Rock 102.5 FM
KCOL NewsTalk 1410 AM
and
Gary Buchanan, president, supporter and friend

. . . and to:
Michael, Susan, Randy, Nina, Terri,
Mark, Carole, Paul, Jim, and Gib,
for each of your contributions.

Contents

Foreword

This is not history as you learned it in school, but it is the true story of the Poudre Valley. If you have ever looked for a book which would give you the complete account of the history of our corner of the world, I'm afraid that you have been disappointed since no such narrative history exists. Most of the history of Fort Collins and Larimer County has been anecdotal in form, with tales of individuals or events that have been told and retold over the years. They are good stories, but they exist in little vacuums with nothing to tie them to the broader tapestry of our history. Actually, the story of the Poudre Valley is like a giant jigsaw puzzle that you start to put together knowing full well that a lot of the pieces have been lost.

The first really serious effort by anyone to record our history was done by a man named Ansel Watrous. He was the editor of the *Fort Collins Courier* newspaper, and he wrote and recorded the daily events and stories about the people of the region for over 30 years. He knew that a record of the early events of Fort Collins, from the time of the military reservation through the founding of the city of Fort Collins and the lives all of the important people who spread their shadows across the land, needed to be told before they were lost and the trail was so badly marred that they were unrecoverable. Pioneers make very poor record keepers; they are too busy trying to stay alive. Watrous kept hoping that somebody would step forward and write this history, but nobody did. Finally, in 1910, Watrous wrote his monumental *History of Larimer County*, which is over 500 pages long.

It is fashionable these days to pooh-pooh Watrous as being a sloppy historian who got too much wrong to be taken seriously. If you want to know what I think, I'm amazed that such a detailed record of ANY kind survives the wild and woolly 19th century. Besides, Watrous got most of the history correct, and what he didn't he was very honest about saying so. In his Preface to the *History of Larimer County*, Watrous states that he worked hard to make the book as accurate as possible, but that he felt very unworthy in writing any kind of a history. Believe me, I know now just how he felt.

It was Watrous himself who gave me the heart and the desire to do this work. When I finally sat down and said, "This is the day that I will begin to write the book", I read the Preface to the History again. The last thing that Watrous wrote was this:

"*Let him who writes the next history of Larimer County enlarge upon the theme and clothe the facts in literary raiment of enchanting beauty and indulge in philosophical comments to his heart's content; it is enough for me that I have furnished the basis for him to build on.*"

Well, I don't know about the literary raiment or enchanting beauty, but I will suppose he wrote those words to me. And so, I begin.

The "Visions" Story

The story of Fort Collins, Larimer County and the Poudre Valley grew over the years as I told it, but how it all came to be and ended up with this book is a story in itself.

In 1976, during the Bi-Centennial Year, I thought it would be a great idea to do a one hour, old-time radio drama on KCOL. My idea was to do a drama on the flood of the river in 1864 that caused Fort Collins to be located where it is today. I went to the library to do a little research. Here I found history, all right. It was contained in a very huge book with 500 pages and teeny-weenie type, by some guy named Ansel Watrous. There was no way I was going to struggle through all *that!* What I ended up with were a couple of pamphlets and a magazine story of the type the Chamber of Commerce puts out.

Armed with such reliable research material, I sat down and wrote an hour-long radio drama. It had spectacular sound effects, music, character parts and production. It was an exciting story and it won all sorts of broadcast awards. Let me tell you that the only good thing about that drama, from an historical standpoint, was the name of the piece. I called it "Visions Along the Poudre Valley". Otherwise, it bore very little resemblance to the facts of what really happened.

Fifteen years later, I was on a sales call for a new radio station, the Eagle, 96.1 FM. On this day I visited with Gib McGarvey, the owner of the venerable Charco-Broiler Restaurant. I wanted Gib to buy some of my advertising. In the course of the conversation, Gib asked if I remembered the radio drama I had done years before and wanted to know what the name of it was. "Visions Along The Poudre Valley," I said.

"Why can't we do something like that," he wanted to know?

"I don't think anybody would be very interested in hearing history on the radio," I said.

Nevertheless, that's what he wanted, so I went back to the radio station and explained the conversation to the station manager, Gary Buchanan. He listened to me and then said,

"Let me see if I've got this right. You want me to take a big hunk of our commercial time, during the 7 o'clock hour in the morning, and give it to you so you can do a history lesson?"

"Yeah, that's about it," I said.

"Well, that's nuts," said Gary.

"That's what Gib wants," I said.

"OK," said Gary, "write up something and record it for me to listen to."

So, in the summer of 1991, "Visions Along the Poudre Valley" went on the air with the Charco-Broiler as the original sponsor. Four years later, the program runs three times a day on three radio stations and is the most popular feature in northern Colorado radio.

Three years ago, I was talking with Tom Byington, president of First State Bank, and one of the original sponsors and supporters of the "Visions" series. Tom told me that he thought I ought to record an audio cassette of the "Visions" series and offer it for sale around town. I thought that was a pretty neat idea, but questioned whether such an audio cassette would be successful.

"Just cut the tape, Phil," he said, "and see what happens."

As they say, the rest is history.

The first Visions audio cassette sold out from one location, Alpine Arts in Old Town Fort Collins. Emboldened by our good fortune, I embarked on a project of recording the entire history of the Poudre Valley and its principal city, Fort Collins, in audio cassette form.

In 1994, we sold nearly 5,000 audio cassettes, and the appetite of the public for more seemed to grow greater everyday. A total of eight audio cassettes have now been written and produced.

I started to be asked to make speeches for groups, service clubs and organizations all over town. It got so I was out speaking a half dozen times a month.

In the back of my head throughout all of this process, was the idea of writing a book. The principal motivation for this was the fact that no complete, narrative history of Fort Collins had ever been written. There are quite a few books about our history, but they are anecdotal in nature. Of course, there was the Ansel Watrous book with its 500 pages. By this time I had acquired a copy of my own and was using it all the time to tell stories about our history. Watrous wrote his book in 1910, and there has been almost a century of history since then.

I should tell you that this entire process has been pushed along by some very good people who have encouraged and supported me. I think its appropriate that I give them credit for the help.

First, are the people I have already mentioned, Gib McGarvey, Tom Byington and Gary Buchanan. Without them, this whole project would have been still-born and never seen the light of day. There have been others. I want to thank Bob Everitt, for seeing this as a good effort in community citizenship and funding large portions of it. Also there was Rick and Linda Roesener, who have been friends for 25 years, and who did just splendid work on the graphics and design of the audio cassettes and the book itself. I can't tell you how many times Rick came wandering into my house and found me staring blankly at a computer screen, and wishing I had never started this time-eating monster that consumed my life. Rick is the guy who doesn't know much about history, but took it as an article of faith that I was getting it right, and encouraged me to continue with the work.

I spent a lot of time in the local history section of the Fort Collins Public Library. I was pushy, impatient and demanding. Yet, in spite of these obvious character flaws, Rheba Massey, the local historian, was gracious, helpful and kind

Of course, I should thank my wife, Jeannie, whose life has been sort of put on perpetual hold over the last four years, and was nice enough to tiptoe past my office and ignore the unsavory sounds that often poured out of the room.

What I wanted was a simple, narrative history of Fort Collins that was organized in a chronological sequence. I wanted the book to be breezy and fun to read, but still contain the true story of our history for the past two centuries. My idea was that people could read the book and, when they were finished, be able to say that they had an appreciation of the history of the Poudre Valley in one, easy to read volume.

I think the reason why the "Visions" series has been so well received is because most of the people who live in Fort Collins today, came here from somewhere else. In fact, about 90% of the town is less than 30 years old. People want to know something about the history of the place where they live. I also think it's important to know what choices previous generations made in order to make better judgments on how we are to proceed in the future.

That volume is now before you, and you can judge for yourself how useful it actually is in understanding our history.

Phil Walker

Part I

"The Awakening"

COLORADO . . . From the Spanish word "Colorar," "to color" with a secondary meaning of "ruddy or blushing". In modern times "Colorado" has come to mean "the color of red", after the red sandstone that is common throughout the state.

The state has an area of 104,247 square miles. It ranks 8th in size of the United States and is larger than all of New England and Ohio combined.

The principal geographic feature of the state is the Rocky Mountains which run 150 miles north and south with a mass that spreads 120 miles east and west to form the Continental Divide of the watershed and 55 of the 200 highest mountains in the world are located within the boundaries of the state.

Four major rivers find their headwaters in Colorado. The Colorado River flows west and is the principal drainage for the entire southwestern United States. The other three rivers the Rio Grande, Arkansas and the South Platte, flow east. These rivers are a part of the vast drainage system that ends with the Mississippi River and the Gulf of Mexico.

In the northern part of the state, a 91-mile-long river flows from the mountains to its confluence with the South Platte . . .

From the mountains of its birth to the plains of the Front Range, the Cache La Poudre River is the source that made it possible for man to make a home in the valley.

Paul Nielsen

How Non-Existent Was My Valley.

For nearly all of the billions of years in which the good-old Earth has been sailing the sea of stars, the Poudre Valley simply did not exist. The valley is a geological "johnny-come-lately". Still, in order for a true history of northern Colorado to make sense, we need to have a basic appreciation of how it came to be.

Some 225 million years ago, all of the land masses of the Earth were concentrated in a single super continent that scientists call Pangaea. Now this land mass was floating around like a cork on a still pond. The pond was a sea of liquid magma, or molten rock, some 50 miles below the surface of the Earth.

Over millions of years this land mass broke apart into identifiable continents which began to drift across the surface of the planet. North America was still connected to the European and Asian land mass as little as 65 million years ago. A picture of northern Colorado at this time would have looked like this . . .

Much of the central plains of North America were covered by a vast inland sea. Northern Colorado would have been at

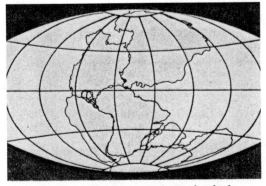

Pangaea. The single, super continent that broke apart 225 million years ago to become the continents of today.

the margin of this sea and a full 5,000 feet lower in elevation. The climate was hot and muggy, actually tropical. Vegetation was abundant and lush. This made the landscape just perfect for the principal animal life that populated the flat plains at that time. Common animals would certainly have included T-Rex, Apatosaurus, Triceritops and the rest of the pantheon of Cretaceous period wildlife.

At approximately 65 million years ago, two enormous subterranean plates crashed into one another beneath the center of the North American plain. This caused the earth to heave and buckle, and the edge of the plates began to shoot into the air, intrusively and violently. The Rocky Mountains were born. When you look to the west and see the mountains, you can tell that most of them were uplifted by plate tectonics and not by volcanic action, even though volcanoes were certainly common enough in the Rocky Mountains. Over millions of years, the mountains were uplifted nearly three miles.

Triceritops along the Poudre. This was just one of the wide range of dinosaurs who lived in northern Colorado, 65 million years ago.
Denver Public Library

Beginning about 15 million years ago, the central expanses of North America underwent a massive dislocation. The entire center of the continent began to rise. The whole land mass, with the mountains sitting on top of it, rose in a long, continuous process that went on for 10 million years until, about 5 million years ago, the central plains had reached 5000 feet above sea level or near their present level of today. That process, by the way, is still in progress, though the changes are barely noticeable. Something on the order of an inch every hundred years.

Nevertheless, it is in this time that a small, short river formed. It was born from the snows of the Rocky Mountains. Over millions of years it carved a canyon from those mountains and flowed out onto the plains to join with other rivers, marching east. In a much later age, it was given the name of Cache La Poudre.

About a million years ago, the Earth began a series of climatological changes that alternately warmed and cooled the planet. When the weather turned cold, the ice sheets from the Arctic began their inexorable march south covering the land with glaciers as much as a mile thick. There have been at least four ice ages, the last one finishing about 11,000 years ago.

In the intervening periods, land bridges formed between North America and Asia via the Bering Strait. This made it possible for animals of all kinds to migrate in both directions, producing some strange outcomes. For example, the horse evolved in North America, right around here. During one of the ice ages, it migrated to Asia and the rest of the world, but disappeared from the New World. It worked the other way as well. We think of the buffalo as being uniquely American, but it evolved in Asia and made its way across the land bridge to at last spill out on the central plains of North America ultimately, to increase to millions of animals.

11,000 years ago, the last ice age was ending. The lands of northern Colorado became green and filled with life.

Buffalo ranged in huge herds of millions of animals. The Poudre Valley was a favorite grazing area. There was plenty of water from the river, and lush grass grew near the river. There were often more buffalo in the Poudre Valley than people in modern Colorado.

Denver Public Library

At the end of the last Ice Age the continental glaciers that had covered the land were receding. That part of the continent south of the Canadian border warmed, and was green and teeming with life. From the Rocky Mountains east to the great rivers, a distance of some thousand miles, the land was like a huge park and was covered with prairie grass three feet tall.

Over this land, nature had fashioned an ecosystem of stupendous proportions. There were all manner of animals of every size and description. Certainly all of the animals we are familiar with today were present. There were deer, elk, mountain lions, moose, coyotes, very large packs of wolves, and, of course, there were the buffalo, upon whom the wolves preyed as the lion does the wildebeest. At times, a single herd of buffalo, containing as many as 50 million individuals would cover the land from horizon to horizon. Some animals that no longer exist today, still remained in small numbers to give color and strangeness to the scenery. They included the giant sloth, the saber-toothed tiger, and the great woolly mammoths.

Man Appears In The Poudre Valley.

Sometime after the last Ice Age had finished, one more animal would make its way across the land bridge of the Bering Strait and begin his migration south, generation upon generation until it reached the skirts of great mountains that look out upon the great plains and the enormous herds of animals that fill it. This was a different kind of animal. It walked on two feet, was clever, used tools, lived in family clans and reasoned about his existence. Man had come to the valley.

His name was Folsom Man. It would not be until the 20th century that we would have the slightest idea that such a primitive man had been present in any of the Western Hemisphere at such an early date. And yet, here he was, following the herds and living a nomadic life.

Since he came from Asia, Folsom Man was of the Mongol stock with the high cheek bones, slanted looking eyes and darker skin. He was quite small. The average man was only about 5 foot 2 inches. The women averaged less than 5 feet. He lived in family clans of 20 to 40 individuals.

Folsom Man had no horses, so he had to hunt the buffalo on foot, and in disguise. Denver Public Library

Periodically, the scattered clans of Folsom Man would gather together in one spot for a time of communal living. These gatherings would serve a number of purposes. A larger group could mount much larger hunting operations to get food to dry and carry the people through the cold winters. There is ample evidence that the hunters would stampede entire herds of animals off cliffs as a simple way of getting a lot of food, in the shortest period of time, with the least effort and danger to the hunters. The gatherings also served the purpose of allowing movement of people from clan to clan through the natural mating process of men and women. There was trading of any number of goods, some of which had traveled a great distance, like shells from the ocean. And finally there was the retelling of stories, experiences and the practice of religious ceremonies.

One of the biggest of these gathering places was along a low ridge of hills north of Fort Collins, just beyond the Rawhide Power plant. At that time the climate must have been cooler with more rain and ground water. This would mean that this land was much more productive and useful than today. There was probably more forest land for firewood, and there were likely much larger herds of animals than we think of as common today. Folsom Man used this campground for many generations. Over the centuries, he left an astonishing number of artifacts in the form of splendid stone points for spears, tools of all kinds and many of the articles that they utilized in their daily lives.

As the climate changed, the campsite was used less and less. The great herds of animals were moving out of the area and the people had no choice but to move with them. Be that as it may, Folsom Man left a rich heritage behind that would fire the imagination of modern man, 10,000 years later

The True Native American

Since the Great Plains were so rich in game, man flourished and his numbers increased. Not that life was easy. It was still dangerous to travel, hunt and just to live. After all, man was

The Spanish were the first white men to explore Colorado. They discovered the Colorado River in 1540.   *Denver Public Library*

still on foot since he had no horses. Man walked and had to carry everything he owned on his back. The herds moved, so he moved, and the centuries passed.

By the time that the white man arrived in the New World with Cortez in 1520, the Native Americans who occupied the Great Plains numbered perhaps 90,000 people . . . all walking. In 1540, Coronado led a three year expedition north from Mexico in search of more golden cities, such as they had found with the Aztecs. Coronado wandered all over the southwest claiming everything in sight for the glory of Spain, including the lands north of the Rio Grande river that he called . . . "Colorado".

None of this had any effect whatsoever on the Indians of the Great Plains. They had their own affairs to pursue. The only thing the white man had that was of interest to the Indians were their horses. And in the last couple of decades of the 16th century, they began to get them in growing numbers.

The horse changed the life of the plains Indians. Now the plains and the great herds of animals could be exploited, because it was now possible to move as fast as the buffalo. This made life on the Great Plains more desirable and soon new tribes of Indians were pressing into Colorado and displacing the tribes that had traditionally lived here. One of the biggest tribes of Indians who got the old heave-ho out of the state were the Apaches. If you thought that the Apaches had always lived down in the barren mountains of Arizona and were the most fierce fighters in the world, then you will be interested to know that the Apaches were defeated and forced out by the Comanches and the Pawnee who arrived from the north. By 1700, the Comanches and the Pawnee were themselves displaced by an even more vigorous and war-like tribe of Indians . . . the Sioux nation, comprising the many Sioux tribes, along with the Cheyenne and the Arapaho.

During the 1700s, the Great Plains, including the Front Range of Colorado and the Poudre Valley, was a vast no-white-man's land. It was surrounded by the mountains on the west, the Spanish in the south, the French in the east at the Mississippi and the British in the north along the Canadian border. Only the tiniest trickle of white pathfinders found their way into the plains to trade with the Indians. These traders were welcomed by the Indians since they brought all sorts of modern artifacts of civilization with them. The foremost of these being weapons. The Indians took to the new weapons, steel knives, rifles, gunpowder and the like with eager zeal since it helped them in their never ending struggles with other tribes and the hated Spanish. Warfare was a way of life for the Indians, and they took great stock in personal bravery, cunning and skill in battle. The great warriors were revered and often were the tribal leaders.

By the beginning of the 19th century, the plains Indians were at their militaristic prime. The French, Spanish and

The tribes of the Plains Indians, numbering perhaps 100,000 people, were the masters of a half million square miles of America's heartland. Denver Public Library

British were scared to death of them, with good reason. Every time they sent an expedition into the Great Plains . . . they were wiped out. The Indians jealously guarded their way of life, customs, religion and a sense of the past, present and future. They never said they owned the land. Instead, they said they belonged to the land and believed they should live in harmony with nature. Until the 1800s really got started, the plains Indians reigned supreme as they had for over 300 years.

A Stirring In The East.

As the 18th century passed, the British were forced out of the eastern part of the continent by the upstart United States of America. The United States had its hands full just taking care of the rather substantial lands they had acquired east of the Mississippi River. But all of that was about to come to a screeching halt because of a war that was being fought in Europe.

Napoleon was in trouble, and he was cash poor. He needed money, specifically gold, to keep up his war effort. Well, the United States had gold, so Napoleon decided to make this little land deal.

Imagine if you will a man who is president and chief operating officer for a great big organization. He sends for a couple of friends who drop by his office. "Fellows," the CEO says, "I bought some land cheap from a guy who needed the money. It was a real good deal, so I bought the land sight unseen. I would like for you to go out and take a look at this land and then come back and tell me what you found." "Sounds simple enough," says one of the fellows, "Exactly where is this land?" The CEO says, "Well, you go out to the Mississippi, turn right and walk for a thousand miles."

In modern terms, that's about the way Merriweather Lewis and William Clark got the job of taking the first organized look at the lands west of the Mississippi in the Louisiana Purchase. This was the largest real estate deal in history. In one fell swoop, and for just 15 million dollars in gold, Thomas Jefferson more than doubled the size of the United States. The new lands amounted to 828,000 square miles. Its eastern boundary was the Mississippi River, but nobody really knew what the western boundary was since nobody really knew what was out there or how far it went. That's why Lewis and Clark were sent. Tucked away in a little corner of this vast territory was a little place called the Poudre Valley.

The Lewis and Clark expedition to explore the lands acquired in the Louisiana Purchase, never made it into Colorado, and so they never saw the Front Range. But their journey all the way to the Pacific Ocean in Oregon and back to civilization fired the imaginations of a lot of people, not the least of which were American presidents. One after another, expeditions went out to further explore the new lands of the West. The first of these to explore Colorado was led by Lt. Zebulon Pike in 1806. He first sighted the mountain which was named for him in November of 1807.

Pike didn't think much of eastern Colorado. He was quick to point out that the land was pretty dry and arid. In fact, in his journal, he wrote, "a barren region, unfit for the habitation of civilized man." Unquote. That didn't sound very inviting at all. As the travelers saying goes, "A nice place to visit, but I wouldn't want to live there." Pike didn't even think it was a nice place to visit, although he did allow that the mountains were quite spectacular and picturesque. The government decided that it all couldn't be so worthless, so they sent other expeditions out to

Stephen Long led an expedition to northern Colorado in 1820. Long's Peak is named for him, even though he never climbed it. The expedition artist drew this picture of the great Poudre Valley.   Denver Public Library

see what they could find. The Indians regarded all this thrashing around with curiosity and wondered if these white men had any clue as to what they were doing.

In 1820 a new expedition was assembled to explore more of the countryside east of the big mountains, under the command of Major Stephen Long. He was supposed to explore the headwaters of the South Platte River. The journey took him close to the mountains and the confluence of the Platte where another unnamed river wandered off to the west. Long explored up the river and finally along the foothills to the Big Thompson canyon that took him to the foot of the mountain that now bears his name . . . Long's Peak.

Not only is Long's Peak a very prominent landmark in these parts, but for your information, the top of Long's Peak is the southwestern corner of Larimer County. Of course it wasn't anything in 1820, and if Stephen Long were to have anything to do with it, it was never going to be anything. On his maps of the all the Great Plains, including Colorado, he wrote four big words . . . "The Great American Desert." That single statement would impede, in fact, nearly stop any progress or development of the Front Range of Colorado for the next 30 years. Other expeditions that explored the Front

Range were equally unimpressed with what they saw. They didn't think that anybody would be able to get anything to grow on the land. It was too dry, and not at all like the land they were used to in the east where everything was green and lush due to an abundance of rainfall. Plus, as everybody had heard, this country was inhabited by a dangerous race of non-white people, and it really was a wilderness . . . barren, useless, with no redeeming virtues and not a truck stop in sight. Most people were unwilling to risk their lives in this hostile land. Luckily, however, most is not all.

The Pathfinders And The Trappers

Some people thought that the idea of a vast unexplored territory was a wonderful challenge, full of adventure and opportunities for riches beyond their wildest dreams. They couldn't wait to go and see for themselves. Private enterprise was slowly prying open the secrets of the West and individuals were working their uncertain ways along the rivers and over the tree-less plains. The magnet that drew them was the fur trade. Beaver pelts were worth a fortune, and there were men willing to pay the price to go get them.

Very few names of the men who first walked across the plains and along the rivers of Colorado are preserved, even in the records of the great fur companies. Mostly they were obscure, illiterate men who owned hardly more than a rifle and their traps. They only appeared amidst the civilized world long enough to sell their pelts and re-supply for a new trip. Sometimes they traveled in groups as part of an expedition organized by the big fur companies. But often they would travel alone, preferring their own company to any others.

In any case, these men lived hard, wild lives, continuously filled with adventure and personal peril. These were the true pathfinders. They were roughly clothed, lived on game, ate anything that didn't eat them first, and were in a constant state of peril. Their average age was 20. Their life expectancy was 21. Most of them were killed or succumbed to disease. But year by year, they dug deeper and deeper into the vast wilderness, seeking out the headwaters of rivers in search of the beaver. Later it would be these men who would become the guides for larger government explorations to follow.

The people of the East and the government were virtually ignoring our western region of the plains. For the first fifty years following the Louisiana Purchase, the people of the East did not have the faintest conception of the immense value of the land they had acquired. Its one considerable attraction was its wealth of beaver fur, and for nearly a half century this was its sole business of importance. The big fur companies that controlled the beaver trade were getting filthy rich on the business. The biggest company was the American Fur Company, owned by John Jacob Astor. When he died in 1848, he was the richest man in America.

It became the practice of the fur companies to bring a measure of civilization and comfort to the free trappers who lived in and near the mountains. A large party would depart from St. Louis in a wagon train filled with supplies, like guns and powder, whiskey, sugar, whiskey, flour, tobacco and whiskey. All of this they would sell for beaver pelts at gatherings that were called *rendezvous*. They were so popular that within just a few years, the rendezvous were drawing as many as 2,000 trappers, Indians, traders and even a few actual tourists. They were a big deal. Everyone loved them and the trappers really whooped it up.

The trapper's rendezvous, put on by the fur companies, were so colorful and so popular that they immediately became on American institution. Trappers, Indians and traders would come for hundreds of miles to spend a few days trading their pelts for provisions for another season, gambling, drinking, playing games . . . all in wild abandonment. When the rendezvous was over, the traders would load up all the beaver pelts they could carry and the wagon train would return to St. Louis with furs to be sold at enormous profits to an eagerly awaiting market.

The Naming Of The River

In November of 1836, a party of trappers and traders, all employees of John Jacob Astor's American Fur Company, were traveling in a wagon train along the foothills, heading north from in front of Long's Peak. They were on there way to a rendezvous to be held on the Green River, over in the vicinity of Flaming Gorge Reservoir on the border between today's

It's easy to imagine a wagon train of trappers, led by a man like Antoine Janis, Sr., on their way to the Poudre Valley in 1836, to camp and give the river the name Cache La Poudre.

Part I: "The Awakening"

23

Colorado and Wyoming. The route was to cross the Big Thompson, cross the Poudre, and then go north to Laramie before turning west to Green River. Of course I'm using the modern names of these places to help you visualize the picture. The trappers didn't even have names for most of the things in this wilderness. It was all just really wild country.

The party of trappers and their wagon train full of supplies for the rendezvous on the Green River made its way along the valley that today is filled with the waters of Horsetooth Reservoir. At the north end of that long valley, you come to the river across a wide lush open area that today is called Pleasant Valley on the north side of Bingham Hill. It was too late in the day to ford the river and so the wagon train made camp and settled in for the night. But overnight a severe snowstorm blew through the valley and in the morning, the wagon train was stuck.

The leader of the party was a French-Canadian by the name of Janis. He was accompanied by his twelve-year-old son, Antoine. Janis gave orders to lighten the load and dig a large pit. It was like a cellar, only bigger. The trappers did everything very carefully. After they had dug the pit, they lined it with pine boughs and animal skins. Then everything that could be spared from each wagon was expertly stored in the pit. A large fire was burned on top of the filled and dirt covered pit to conceal all these supplies from the Indians. Included in the supplies were several hundred pounds of gunpowder. So, the French speaking trappers called this, "The hiding place of the powder" . . . "Cache La Poudre". Now our river had a name.

Some months later, the party returned to the valley and recovered all their supplies. Nothing was lost and nothing remained to show that anyone had ever been there. The valley went back to sleep for almost another decade, with no permanent settlements or even a trace of civilization.

Expansion In The West.

The Front Range of the Rocky Mountains remained largely uninhabited by the white man throughout all of the 1830s, 40s, and 50s. Except for the fur trade, there was just nothing here to really be of much interest to the general population of the East. They believed the stories from the explorers like Stephen

Long who said that all of eastern Colorado was just another part of the Great American Desert . . . dry, barren and useless. Also, there was the not so small matter of those great big mountains in the West. They represented a huge impediment to anyone. They were pretty to look at, but they were a nightmare for travelers.

However, this did not mean that America had given up on coming west to seek their fortunes. Just the opposite was true and the lands of Oregon and California had a great deal of appeal, soon a steady stream of emigrants were making their way to the West Coast via the Oregon Trail. But the main problem with moving west of the Rocky Mountains was that all of that land was claimed and occupied by Mexico. California, for example, had been settled by the Spanish for three centuries. Now it was claimed by Mexico who also claimed Arizona, Utah, Nevada, New Mexico and part of Colorado. To make matters worse, the British claimed territory in the Northwest, principally Oregon and Washington. This made it a little difficult for people to just move west and settle in. By 1845 matters were coming to a head.

In 1845 , a new concept was sweeping the United States. It was called Manifest Destiny. Simply stated, Manifest Destiny said that the American continent should be settled, owned, occupied and exploited by Americans to the exclusion of everybody else. So, in 1845, the United States was able to wrench an agreement from the British for the lands that would become the states of Oregon and Washington and the border was established with Canada, just where it is today. But the Mexicans were not interested in negotiating or selling their territory further south and in 1846 war between the two countries broke out.

By 1848, two important things had occurred. First, the United States had defeated Mexico and won almost all the land it has today, including California. The second thing that happened was that gold was discovered in California and set off the great rush to the coast. This changed everything. Now hundreds of thousands of people got on the trail, headed west. The principal routes they followed were along the Sante Fe Trail to the south of big mountains and the Oregon Trail north of the mountains. In our part of the country there was exactly one area of civilization of any consequence. This was Fort Laramie, which was maintained by the army.

The Oregon Trail brought tens of thousands of pioneers across the country, headed for the gold fields of California and the rich farm lands of the Northwest.

Denver Public Library

Fort Laramie was the principal stopping point for wagon trains headed west. The fort was along the Laramie River about 50 miles north of present day Cheyenne. It had been established in 1836. The wagon trains avoided dealing with the Rocky Mountains by bypassing them altogether. However, it meant that there were at least more people moving through the area, and some of them made their way into northern Colorado and the Poudre Valley. In 1844, 20-year-old Antoine Janis returned to the valley of the Cache La Poudre he had seen as a boy with his father eight years before when they had hidden the gunpowder and named the river.

It was Antoine Janis' intention to stake a claim and make a home in the valley, which he did. This makes Janis the first white settler in the Poudre Valley. He staked his claim in what is now known as Pleasant Valley. That is the gorgeous land that lays just on the other side of Bingham Hill. Janis had made his own personal treaty with the Indians and according to him, he now owned all the land. Pretty soon, other trappers, explorers, and travelers had begun to congregate along the river. They used the area as a camp ground and headquarters to conduct their trapping and trading operations. They were certainly there in 1847 when the Mormons, with their long wagon trains, drawn by weary, footsore beasts and travel stained but hopeful men, women and children passed through on their way to the Great Salt Lake Basin.

Emigrants who were moving west toward the gold fields of California and the rich farm lands of Oregon traveled along the easiest and safest routes they could find. Foremost in travel of this kind was to stay as close as possible to water in this arid country. It was pretty obvious they needed water to drink and grass for the stock to graze on. So the trails kept them close to the rivers. This meant that many of the wagon trains traveled along the South Platte to the Poudre River and then north from Laporte into Wyoming before turning west again. It was the route the Mormons and a good many other settlers.

In 1848, a band of Cherokee Indians, headed for the gold fields in California, traveling along the South Platte to Cherry Creek near the site of present day Denver. They did a little prospecting along Cherry Creek and found some gold, but didn't stay very long as they continued on to California in search of the greater prize. They went north along the front range and then on to Wyoming where they joined the Oregon trail for the rest of the trip west. The route they used would be called the Cherokee Trail for many years. Today, that same route is better known by various names including Highway 287 and Overland Trail. People were beginning to move into our part of the world.

In 1852, a man by the name of Todd passed through our valley as he was crossing the continent. This is how he described it in his journal: "The waters of the river were crystal clear all the way down to the Platte. The waters were full of trout. The undulating bluffs slopped gently down to the valley which was carpeted with the most luxuriant grasses. The whole valley was black with buffalo as thick as bees in a hive. The days were pleasant, the nights cools, and the mornings crisp and bracing. The sky was a deep, rich blue, tinted golden in the morning and evening, like a dream of beauty.

Not an ax had marred the symmetry of the groves of trees that grew along the river. Not a plow or hoe had ever broken its virgin soil. Wild flowers of the richest hue beautified the landscape, while above all towered the majestic Rocky

Mountains in the west, like the grim sentinels they are . . . ever watching . . . watching and noting this advancing vanguard of civilization." Todd went on across the continent in search of gold and glory, but in the end he returned to the valley that had so impressed him as it was soon to impress others, and it was here that he made his home. It didn't look much like the Great American Desert to him.

The 1850s drifted by for northern Colorado, indeed for the entire Front Range, while the floods of immigrants rushed past us on the north along the Oregon Trail in the wild rush to the West Coast and California and Great Northwest. In the Poudre Valley, the only settlement whatsoever was the tiny collection of trappers and traders that came and went from the place that they called La Porte, another French word that means, "The Gateway". There could not have been more than a hundred white men in the entire valley. Their neighbors were the Arapaho and Cheyenne Indian tribes with whom they were at peace.

The Colorado Gold Rush

All of that was about to change dramatically. In July of 1858, a party of prospectors arrived at the Cherry Creek near where Denver is today. These were the same Cherokee Indians who had prospected there in 1848 but had gone on to California. Now they had finished their expedition to California, returned to Georgia and reorganized another prospecting party to come back to Colorado to look some more. Included in the group were two white men named Russell and Green, so of course, it became known as the Russell/Green expedition. The party of Georgians prospected Cherry Creek and the Platte, and they came up with $500 worth of gold, about two handfuls. Now that's not really a fortune, even by 1858 standards.

Nevertheless, the simple fact that *any* gold had been discovered was like a little pebble thrown into a still pond. The ripples went on and on and on. By the time the story got to the eastern newspapers, the amount of gold actually discovered had grown from two handfuls to the size of the Great Pyramid and furthermore it was just sitting there waiting for you to go chisel off a nice hunk for yourself . . . free! Maybe I'm exaggerating the story just a little, but the result was the same and the rush was on.

Within just a few months, thousands of prospectors, miners, traders and fortune hunters poured into Colorado. The first stage reached Denver City in May of 1859 after having made the trip from Leavenworth, Kansas, a distance of 687 miles in 45 days. The cost of a ticket on the Concord Coach was $100, including meals. Soon other discoveries were made. Silver was discovered in the mountains west of Denver in 1860, and the rush turned into a fever. The Front Range of Colorado, and the mountains themselves were now viewed in somewhat less forbidding terms. More properly stated, the risks were the same, but the possibility of gain was now considerably higher and made the risk worth taking.

Settlement Begins In The Poudre Valley.

Of course, not everybody who came west with Pikes' Peak or Bust painted on his wagon found any gold or silver. Also, a fair number of people who came to the Front Range of Colorado were here for other reasons beyond mining for the precious stuff. All of these people out here had to eat, didn't they? Well of course they did! And they couldn't very well ship all the food they would need a thousand miles, could they? Well, of course not! So that meant that the food would have to be grown locally, and imbedded in the hordes of gold-seekers were the true pioneers — the farmers and ranchers.

Now the true value of the Poudre Valley was realized, which was that the land itself was the richest, most fertile soil that anyone had ever seen. If they could figure out a way to get enough water on to that land, it would become the wonder of the continent. Most of the people who came were single men, young, strong and ambitious . . . men who owned their own shadows. The few who had families in the East had left them to come later when their husbands and fathers had built homes and established a beachhead from which the family could make a stand against anything out here on the wild frontier. The pioneers spread out through the valley, staking squatter's claims.

The pioneers who came to the Poudre Valley beginning in 1859, congregated around the old trapper's camp that had become known as Laporte, French for "The Gateway". That was the correct name for Laporte, because it truly was the gateway to all of the thousands of square miles north of Denver and the South Platte River. It was the portal, through the Poudre Canyon, to North Park and the Continental Divide. And it was the jumping off point for access to the north and the route to Fort Laramie. Between 1858 and 1860 the community of Laporte grew rapidly and a town company called the Colona Company was organized, with a purpose to build a city on the banks of the Cache La Poudre.

By 1861, when the first territorial legislature of Colorado met, Laporte had 50 or 60 log cabins, several businesses and was the most important center of commerce north of Denver. So when the legislature carved up the territory into counties, Laporte was designated the County Seat of Larimer County. In those early days, Laporte was a bustling business and supply center for immigrants. One of the most important elements of Laporte's success was that in 1862, the Overland Stage began operations along the front range from Denver to Fort Laramie and Laporte was a main home station along the line, established a regular line of communications for mail and passengers. A toll bridge was built over the Poudre River and an avalanche of emigrants heading west flowed in an endless stream across it. Ansel Watrous reported that the wagon trains stretched out farther than the horizon and that in a single day as many as 200 wagons paid $5 a piece to cross the river.

The Overland Stage became a very important link with the civilized world in the absence of the railroad or hardly any roads. The stage was the prime mover, which unfortunately made it the prime target for attacks by Indians, outlaws, and the natural dangers of the wild country. A high priority was placed on protection for the Overland Stage as well as the several hundred emigrants who now were living in the Poudre Valley.

Jack Slade, The Poudre Valley Legend.

The history of the American West is filled with stories about men who made their marks on the land with guts, gunfire and gore. These stories are imbedded into our culture and our souls. People never seem to tire of hearing them and the closer to home they are, the better.

Jack Slade is the man on the left. Virginia Dale Slade, for whom the stage station was named, is in the window and three members of Slade's gang are on the right.

Fortunately we have a wonderful character. His name is not as famous as Billy the Kid or Wyatt Earp, but it should be. He was as reckless and as notorious as any of them. His name was Jack Slade, and in less than two years he managed to become a part of our history, forever. It is a tale of high adventure on the high plains of Colorado.

Jack Slade was born in Illinois, sometime before 1830. When he was 13 years old, he had already developed a reputation for an uncontrollable temper. He killed a man who was bothering him and his school friends by hitting him in the head with a rock. Slade's father, an Illinois Congressman, was able to get the boy out of town and into Texas where he was a volunteer in the Mexican War in 1848. While he was in Texas, Slade met and married the woman who would remain with him for the rest of his life. She was the voluptuous and lively Virginia Dale, a woman of handsome features even though she weighed in at 160 pounds on a tall frame. She also had a rather unlovely character and was forever interfering in her husband's business. In fact, a lot of her troubles seem to have originated with her. Well, this sweet couple left Texas and headed for the Front Range of Colorado in 1858.

Part I: "The Awakening"   31

Slade became an employee of Ben Holladay's Overland Stage Company and had an important job as a division chief. This meant that his job was to make sure that nothing . . . NOTHING, interfered with the movement of passengers, mail or freight on the Overland Stage. The stage line was the delicate umbilical to the civilized world which it maintained in a network across the vast expanses of the wild frontier. Its reliability was its great value and Slade gave them that in spite of all obstacles. His single-minded efforts were very much appreciated by the stage line and he was valued as a man who could get the job done and bring the stages through on time and intact. This, in spite, of hostile Indians, bandits and other ruffians who wandered the West in search of easy prey. The main problem, besides his terrible temper, was that Slade drank; and when he was drunk, he was capable of anything . . . even murder.

Soon after arriving on the job for the Overland Stage, Slade killed a man named Andrew Farrar. The two of them had been drinking heavily in a saloon out of Green River, Wyoming and were having an animated conversation in which something was said about shooting. Slade said that, "No man must ever dare him to shoot." Whereupon Farrar said, "I dare you to shoot me." So Slade pulled out his revolver and shot the man right in the chest. He was instantly sorry for what he had done and sent a man on a fast horse to Fort Bridger for a doctor. Slade took care of Farrar until the doctor arrived, but it did no good, as Farrar died anyway.

What do you suppose the stage line did about this? Nothing. They viewed Slade's private life as his own and didn't care what he did as long as he was performing a valuable service for them. So Slade got away with the killing and his reputation began to grow.

With the discovery of gold in the Colorado mountains in 1858, thousands of people began to move into the Front Range. The most popular route was from a fork in the Oregon Trail in Nebraska and down along the South Platte River to Denver City and the gold fields to the west.

Right on the border of Colorado and Nebraska was a trading post that was run by a man named Jules Reni, a French Canadian, who had been trading with the Indians, but now found it more profitable to trade with the immigrants heading west. Reni named his trading post and way stop for the wagon trains Jules . . . burg. Not long after, the Overland Stage established a home station at Julesburg to take advantage of this profitable trade with pioneers. Slade was put in charge of this new section of the line and proceeded to improve the quality of all the services by upgrading the livestock, personnel and stage stations.

This put him into immediate conflict with Reni, who had turned his trading post into a hot bed for wild times, loose women and unfair treatment of travelers. On one occasion, Slade came to Reni's ranch and found horses there that belonged to the Overland Stage, which he confiscated. Jules Reni swore vengeance and disliked Slade intently.

In the spring of 1860, Slade rode into the stage station where Jules was living. Jules saw that Slade was unarmed, so when Slade started to enter the combination general store and bar, Jules came running out shooting. He hit Slade with all six shots from his pistol. Unsatisfied with that, he ran home and got a shotgun and emptied both barrels of buckshot into the helpless Slade. Satisfied that he had finished the job, Reni told a couple of bystanders, "When he is dead, you can put him in one of those dry goods boxes and bury him." Slade looked up from the ground and said, "I'll live long enough to wear your ears on my watch chain." With that Jules laughed.

Just at that moment, the Overland Stage rolled into the station with the superintendent of the line aboard. Upon seeing what Jules had done, he ordered his men to hang him, which they did. But they didn't kill him, even though his face turned black. The superintendent agreed to spare Reni's life if he would promise to leave the territory and never come back. Reni agreed to this, and they let him go.

Slade was mortally wounded. He was not expected to live. The surgeon from Fort Laramie rode 167 miles to tend to the wounded Jack Slade, and the surgeon removed a handful of lead from his body.

But Slade did not die. After a long period of convalescence, he returned to his job with the Overland Stage. The company promoted him to chief of the Rocky Mountain division. On the way back into the frontier from St. Louis, where Slade has gone to seek the help of a good doctor, he sent word ahead that he would shoot Reni on sight, but that he wouldn't go out of his way to look for him. Jules got the message and sent word out that he was going to come looking for Slade and finish the job.

A deadly confrontation was a sure bet. Jules Reni knew it. Jack Slade knew it. The whole territory knew it. Slade went to Fort Laramie to get some advise. The army garrison at Fort Laramie was the only real law in the entire region. The officers agreed that something would have to be done since Jules had threatened to kill Slade. The commander of the post at Fort Laramie, a fellow with the familiar sounding name of Lt. Colonel William O. Collins, basically told Slade that he would approve of any action that Slade took.

With this endorsement, Slade sent men down the stage line in search of Jules Reni. They found him at the second stage station they searched and took Jules into custody, tied him up, and sent word back up the line to Slade. Slade arrived on the next stage and found Reni all bundled up at the Chansau station just across the Wyoming border.

This is the spot at which the legend begins . . . that tiny kernel of truth that grows, over the years into something that doesn't much resemble the real truth. Of course, these add-on, fanciful twists to a tale, DO, make them a lot more fun to listen to. That's where we got stories like Robin Hood and King Arthur, and Ali Baba and the Forty Thieves.

For example, in Mark's Twain's book, *Roughing It*, Twain devotes two whole chapters to the same incident I am about to tell. They're not even close to each other in the facts. However, I would submit that Mark Twain's writing is a whole lot more meaningful in spirit than mine will ever be. This is also the reason why Mark Twain's writing is in every library in the world, whereas I am delighted if mine makes it through the next season at the dentist's office.

Anyway, Jack Slade rolled into the Chansau Station in a red heat. He found Jules Reni all trussed up like a baked ham and tied to a corral post. A lot of the stories say that Slade didn't dawdle at his revenge for more than a minute and that he promptly shot Reni, once in the mouth and once right between the eyes.

Another bunch of stories has Slade playing the mean-spirited executioner. This would certainly have been the case if Slade had made an alcoholic transformation on the stage from

Fort Laramie. In these more colorful stories, Slade takes a drink from a bottle and then announces to Reni that "this time, I'm going to put a bullet in your leg, or shoot off your thumb," and other lines to that effect. Over the period of some time, Slade systematically shoots Reni to pieces.

In any case, Reni was killed and Slade was the one that did it. And there is one other fact that has never been in dispute. When Reni was dead, Slade announced to everyone that he was fulfilling his vow to wear Reni's ears on his watch chain. Then he took out his knife, cut off the ears, and did, in fact, wear them on his watch chain. Hardly anyone missed this feature since the rotting ears put off an ungodly stench.

Now, to resume the story of the stagecoaches. The Overland Stage put in a new line that was to run along the foothills, north from Denver to Laporte, the only center of commerce in northern Colorado, and continue north along what is now mostly Highway 287 ending at Fort Laramie, north of today's Cheyenne. At this time there were no cities of Laramie or Cheyenne. There was just Denver, Laporte and Fort Laramie and all the rest of it was a wide open wilderness.

Into this garden spot rode Jack Slade and Virginia Dale. Slade had come to take over this part of the Overland Stage line and get it open from Denver to Fort Laramie. The first thing he did was to build a new home station about 25 miles north of Laporte to serve as an overnight stop for passengers and a place to change horses. It was in a glade with plenty of space, water and grass for the livestock, and it was about a days travel by stage from Laporte. He called the station Virginia Dale in honor of his wife. So it remains today and is preserved in nearly completely authentic condition by an active historical society.

But in 1862, it was a busy and vital link in the stage route that ran along the foothills. Jack Slade was the master of it all. He certainly was very good at keeping the stages moving on schedule and reasonably safe. In fact, he could have been a great civilizing influence on the whole area. Alas, he threw it all away in bouts of outrageously drunken behavior. His reputation did not suffer, however. Even in the East, people had heard of Jack Slade, and when they got to his part of the line in their journeys west, they were all anxious to catch a glimpse of him. Often enough he cheerfully obliged.

One day, in the fall of 1862, Slade set out on an inspection tour of his far-flung empire. When he got to Laporte, he got roaring drunk. Slade then piled all the passengers onto the stage and galloped out of Laporte, leaving the bewildered driver standing on the road in the dust.

Slade drove the stage wildly and luggage flew off in all directions. When the startled passengers began to complain, Slade drew his revolver and started blasting away on the roof of the stage, into the passenger compartment. All four of the people bailed out, and then stood in the prairie, dusting themselves off as the stage rumbled out of sight with the hoots of Slade's laughter, ringing across the foothills

Slade drove the stage and the team into the Big Thompson station, near where Loveland is today, on a dead run. He jumped down in a cloud of dust and marched into the station house. Here he met the station master, a man named Boutwell, and demanded a drink. When Boutwell didn't move fast enough to suit Slade, he grabbed a double-barreled shotgun and shoved it in his face. Then he had Boutwell fix him up a concoction that was made . . . "just so." Poor Mr. Boutwell had to mix the drink several times because his hands were shaking so much that he kept spilling it. Finally he got it and looked into Slade's brooding, black eyes. "Put it on the end of the gun," said Slade. Boutwell carefully placed the glass on the end of the shotgun, which was stuffed up his nose. Well, Slade just laughed and tossed down the drink in one gulp. Then he laughed again and went back to the stage with its sweating horses, and took off in a cloud of dust.

Slade drove the stage on to the next station on the Little Thompson River a few miles further south. He drove wildly and by the time he got to the station, one of the horses collapsed in exhaustion. The man at the station came running out and started to unhitch the horses. Slade made some profane remark and the man answered with something like, "only a mad man would drive horses like this."

BLAM! the poor man was suddenly struck to the ground from behind, and when he turns to look, he is staring down the bore of a gigantic revolver, wielded by an enraged Jack Slade.

"Who are you?" says Slade, "You don't work for me."

"Right, right, I don't. My name is Frank Bartholf. I just got here from the East to help out my brother-in-law here at the station. You must be Jack Slade. My brother-in-law told me to expect you."

"It's a good thing," growled Slade, " 'cause I don' allow none of my men to sass me."

Bartholf beat a hasty retreat, but Slade was in rare form. He raged around the station and came upon two men camped out by the stable. Slade had his gun drawn, so the men scrambled to their feet and drew their guns. Slade evily threatened to shoot one of their horses. The men talked him out of that. So Slade shot their dog, which was quietly sleeping under a wagon. Then Slade kicked over the pot of coffee on the fire and stormed off.

All of this time, the men stood there, with their guns drawn, perfectly capable of defending themselves . . . and their dog. But they didn't. They were too terrified to move a muscle. Jack Slade cast a long shadow in these parts.

Oddly enough, Jack Slade hated it when his stage drivers got drunk. He wasn't going to have them wrecking the stages and injuring passengers. Well, once a driver did get drunk and did wreck a stage and injure passengers. Slade found out that the driver was sold the liquor by Adna Chaffee, the store-keeper in Laporte. Slade sent word that Chaffee was not to sell any more liquor to his men. Adna Chaffee was no shrinking violet — few of the pioneers were — and he sent back word to Slade that "just because he'd killed Jules Reni and chopped off his ears, it didn't mean that he was afraid of him and that he would sell liquor to anyone he pleased."

Two nights later, Slade arrived on the stage from Virginia Dale with three of his henchmen. They all got outrageously drunk and burst into Chaffee's store. Quickly they tied the frightened shopkeeper to a center post and then proceeded to shoot the place to pieces, spilling vinegar, molasses, flour and sugar all over the floor and then slid through the gooey mess while they continued to blast away. After a while, they tired of their fun and with a bullet fired over the head of Chaffee, they went out of the store laughing.

But that wasn't the end of it. A few days later, Slade came back to the store and plunked down $800 to pay for all the damages he had done. He was sober this time. However, as he left, he said to Adna, "This is to pay for the damages, but the next time I tell you not to sell liquor to my men, you'll know I mean it."

Finally, even Slade's good work in running the stage line is not enough to keep the company from deciding that they could get along without such a colorful and dangerous fellow. The hijacking of a gold shipment that was payroll for the soldiers at Fort Laramie was the last straw. It amounted to $60,000 in gold coins (about a million dollars today) and the money was never found, even though it was taken by masked men only a mile from the Virginia Dale station. The stage line suspected Slade of being the master mind for the holdup, but they couldn't prove it. So they just fired him.

Everybody expected trouble that summer of 1863, and the replacement chief for the stage line was happy for the job, but the last thing he wanted was to have to be the man to tell Slade face-to-face that *he* was the one who was replacing him. But it was an anti-climax. Slade went very meekly. Quite uncharacteristic of him. Maybe he was tired of the job. Or, maybe he had all the money he needed.

At any rate, Slade and Virginia Dale took off for a gold strike in Virginia City, Montana, where Slade continued his drunken ways. Unfortunately for him, he went to a town where he had no authority with a stage line, and the people in Virginia City were only slightly less evil than he was.

Slade got into one drunken brawl after another. He actually did a tremendous amount of damage to stores and property. Finally when the vigilante committee of Virginia City had enough, they ordered Slade to be taken out and hung. It was the morning of March 10, 1863.

The crowd took Slade out into the street, and there were tense minutes of argument with Slade's few friends. But the vigilantes were adamant. They were not going to let Slade go. They were not going to let him see his wife, and if his friends did anything about it, they were all going to be shot. With that Jack Slade was tied hands and feet and stood up on a dry goods box. A noose was placed around his neck. Then the box was kicked away and Slade swung down, his boots barely scraping the ground. It took him 30 minutes to die.

Shortly thereafter, Virginia Dale came pounding into town on horseback. Seeing what the crowd had done, she profanely cursed them all. The crowd was in no mood to put up with anymore nonsense, and they told Virginia Dale that if she was not out of town with her husband in ten minutes and never come back, then they would string her up too.

Virginia Dale took her husband's body all the way to Salt Lake City, where she buried him. He remains there today.

So ended the life of Jack Slade. He was less than 40 years old. He was a real life desperado, and now has become a permanent part of our history.

The Military Arrives In The Poudre Valley.

Protecting the valley and the Overland Stage was not all that easy. In 1861, the United States blew up in Civil War, right in the middle of all this western expansion. With the coming of the war, most of the regular army troops were needed for more serious fighting in the east. So most of them pulled out. The Indian tribes of the plains seized on this opportunity to declare a war of their own against the settlers with a main purpose to annihilate every white in sight and reclaim all their territory. And they had the manpower to do it in northern Colorado. In the whole Poudre Valley, including Laporte there could not have been more than 300 people. The Indians would be able to field a force of 1,000 fighters — serious threats indeed.

Throughout most of the 1860s, The Indians were a very real threat to the people of northern Colorado. With the reassignment of most of the regular troops for the armies of the East for the Civil War, the settlers of the Poudre Valley were on their own to protect themselves as best they could, and the situation was grim indeed. And northern Colorado was not unique. All over Colorado, the Indians were raiding everywhere. They cut the supply lines in a dozen places. They attacked settlements, ran off horses and cattle and killed many pioneers. The Overland Stage was forced to suspend operations, and the wagon trains ground to a halt.

The territorial government spent almost all its time and money trying to raise a volunteer cavalry to protect its people. Finally, in the fall of 1863, Company B, of the First Colorado Volunteer Cavalry was sent to Laporte to patrol the Overland Stage line and protect the lives and property of the settlers. The soldiers established their encampment on the bottom lands, near the river on Antoine Janis' claim. It was almost exactly in the same location that Antoine Janis father had stopped his wagon train of supplies 27 years before. Log cabins for the officers and some of the men and stables for the horse were built and Company B, settled in for the winter.

The winter of 1863 was the worst that anyone could remember. Even the Indians spoke of its harshness and severity. Earlier than usual, about the middle of October, big storms began to pile up along the Front Range and in the mountains, and it began to snow. It snowed and snowed and snowed, filling the gulches and ravines in the mountains several feet deep. The snow was six feet deep in the timber on the hillsides. Altogether an immense quantity of water making material was accumulating. All the way through Christmas and into January of 1864, there was always a deep cover of snow on the ground around Laporte.

It was a terrible winter, storm after storm swept through the valley. Out on the plains to the east, wagon trains were ground to a halt and supply wagons were abandoned. The stages could normally get through when nothing else was moving. Now, even the stages stopped running after several of them became lost in the furious blizzards and had wandered about wildly on the trackless prairies. Company B of the Colorado Volunteer cavalry were immobilized just like everyone else. Fortunately, the endless bad weather made their services unnecessary since the Indians were passing the time quietly in their lodges. In the end, everyone just hunkered down and waited for the awful winter to end.

With the coming of spring, 1864, the settlers of the Poudre Valley had mixed emotions. The winter was over and the prospects for a good growing season for their crops lay ahead. But also the end of winter meant the resumption of renewed attacks by marauding Indians and the not inconsiderable danger from outlaws, horse thieves and murderers. To make matters worse, Company B of the First Colorado Volunteer Cavalry pulled out of Laporte in April and that made everyone nervous. The entire area was relieved to learn that the regular army at the big garrison in Fort Laramie had been ordered to take up the job of protection.

The commanding officer at Fort Laramie was also the commander of the troops of the 11th Ohio Cavalry. His name was

Lt. Colonel William O. Collins. He was a highly respected officer and regarded by his superiors as a man who was able to protect the settlers, and their property. And the Indians trusted him as well, as a man who kept his word. Colonel Collins sent two companies of his 11th Ohio, to Laporte to take up the job of protecting the stage line, the settlers and the increasingly valuable Poudre Valley.

But spring was also dawning in other places as well. In the East, new waves of immigrants were getting set to embark on the long journey of a thousand miles across the Great Plains.

Oceans Of Grass

It was unusually warm for spring. A robust sun shone brightly and made it humid, almost sultry, over Rockford, Illinois. The city bustled with people and carriages moving about their business. The solid buildings and spacious homes of this prosperous midwestern city stood in stark contrast to the tiny caravan of two wagons with the usual canvas cover of all "prairie schooners" that waited on a quiet street for depar-

Sarah Milner and her family traveled by wagon train from Rockford, Illinois to the Front Range. The journey took 12 weeks. Huge trains with hundreds of wagons were common in the early 1860's, all bound for Colorado territory and the gold fields.

Denver Public Library

ture into the vast, unknown wilderness that waited just a few miles to the west.

Joseph Milner stood at the front of his little expedition with its two yokes of oxen hitched to each wagon. He was having a few last words with friends and business associates.

"Joseph," said one, "I wish that I could have talked you out of this dangerous gamble. Doesn't it occur to you that you are taking an awful chance by trying to move your entire family across nearly a thousand miles of uncharted wilderness, alone, and with no prospects of success even if you get all the way to Colorado territory?"

Milner shook his head, "My son, William, writes that the gold fields of Colorado offer great opportunities for wealth and prosperity. He says that men are taking a fortune in gold from the mines everyday."

"Maybe," said his friend, "But you are betting everything you have, and the lives of your family on a dangerous speculation."

One of the others, who had been the family doctor for years, said, "And besides, Joseph, your daughter Sarah is too weak to make this journey. She's not going to last a month out there in that wilderness."

"She'll make it," said Milner stubbornly. "One of my other sons says that the climate in the Colorado Territory is much better than here. He says that they have something called "Chinook Winds", that blow warm air across the mountains and melt the snow and dry the air."

"Poppycock!" said the doctor. "Your daughter has been an invalid all her life. It's a thousand miles, Joseph! She'll grow sick and slow you down to a crawl."

The object of this conversation, 19-year-old Sarah, sat on the seat of the second wagon with her mother, Ann Milner. "I suppose the doctor is telling Papa that I'm not well enough to make the journey," she pouted.

"You'll make it, Sarah," comforted her mother, "We all will."

Joseph Milner shook hands with his friends and they all wished him good fortune and God's grace. He turned to the wagons and made one last check of his inventory. There were two wagons, piled high with all the provisions that the family would need, both on the trail and in the new lands in the

West. Each wagon would be pulled by four sturdy oxen. There were also two cows to provide fresh milk along the way and to help out for the heavy pulls or to be spares in case one or more of the oxen should die or become crippled. His family waited quietly on the wagons or standing next to them. Altogether the party numbered eight. There was Joseph and Ann Milner, four of their sons, Joseph Jr., Matthew, James and Benjamin, a Mrs. Reeves, who was traveling west to live with her sons who were working the gold mines near Central City, and there was Sarah. She sat bravely on the wagon and looked to the west with hopeful eyes.

It was Wednesday, April 6, 1864, when the Milner family pulled out of Rockford and headed west. For the first few days, the land about them seemed familiar and comforting. But with each passing day, the countryside grew more sparsely settled and the roads became a single trail, and the trail meandered in an aimless ribbon toward the setting sun.

Joseph Milner had planned to make the trip in a leisurely fashion, partly on account of Sarah, and partly to provide plenty of time for the oxen to graze. No extra feed had been brought along for the stock and the Milners expected them to eat their way across the plains. Each day the family would stop anytime after mid-afternoon where a good campsite could be found. The Milner family was deeply religious and would not travel at all on Sundays. The family would look for a school house or the like on Saturday since religious services were almost certainly to be held in any school house in a thinly populated region of America at that time. These the family always attended.

Each day when the family stopped they would unload a large tent that would be erected for the four boys to sleep. The parents slept in one of the wagons and Sarah slept in the other wagon with Mrs. Reeves. The family also would unload a cook stove and a large table and chairs for the entire party.

The emigrants moved across Illinois. Grass and water were plentiful for the oxen and they grew fat and frisky. The party had not been on the road for two weeks when, on a long down grade, the animals all became very unruly and unmanageable. Both wagons hurtled wildly across the open prairie and all of the camp supplies were thrown out the back of the lead wagon and were run over by the second wagon. When the men finally got the teams back under control and back to the place where everything had been tossed out, the family found that their table and chairs had all been smashed to kindling and the medicine chest that had been so carefully prepared to take care of Sarah had been completely destroyed. However, Sarah had seemed to grow stronger with each passing day and had no need of any medicine, so the supplies were never missed.

A severe drought prevailed throughout Iowa as the pioneers passed through the state. Water and grass for the oxen was scarce. Nearly every farm had posted a sign saying, "No water for oxen." At times the party was forced to scoop water out of the tracks of passing animals with spoons to get enough for drinking their noon tea. On one occasion, a gust of wind blew dirt into Sarah's tea.

"Shall I never have a clean cup of tea again," she said in disgust as she threw it out!"

Brother Joe laughed, "When we get to Colorado, the wind will blow our pancakes off the griddle, and we shall have to chase them."

"Joe Milner," grumbled Sarah, "Just because you have been across this prairie before, doesn't mean that you know everything!"

"I know that it will get much more dangerous before it gets better," answered young Joe. "Wait until you see your first Red Indian." Sarah cringed, "Oh Joe, will be really see Indians? Are they fierce? Shall I be ravaged?" "Not if we are careful . . . and lucky," replied Joe. "When we come to their hunting grounds on the plains of Nebraska, there will be troops from the army to protect us."

True to Joe's prediction, before the little band had reached central Nebraska ugly rumors began to be heard from the teamsters on the big freight wagons heading back to the East. Small parties, such as the Milner's, were being attacked and murdered along the trail. The men talked about huge war parties of Indians gathering in western Nebraska. The days grew tense, the nights long.

When Sarah's family reached an army fort in the middle of Nebraska, they were held up until fifty wagons had arrived to make the rush to Colorado safer. Further orders were given by the army for all wagons to halt at Julesburg until a hundred had been assembled before going on to Denver and the Front Range.

Now a long line of wagons, in picturesque fashion, wound across the plains. A hot, desert sun beat down on the rolling wagons. Sarah Milner sat inside her wagon as it bounced and jolted along. With so many supplies piled in the wagon, she was just inches from the top of the canvas. She found this very trying and uncomfortable.

A young man, who had joined the wagon train at the army post, road up along her wagon on a little burro. "Howdy, maam," he said. "You look real hot inside that wagon. Why don't you come on down and ride my burro. He don't take too good to the full weight of a man, but he'll carry you with no trouble." After a slight nod from her father, Sarah hopped out of the wagon and changed places with the man on his burro. For a number of days thereafter, Sarah found a great freedom on her burro and would range far and wide of the wagons for the illusion of solitude. There was so much to see out on the wild prairie new and beautiful or interesting to a young girl who had been sheltered as an invalid in the crowded valleys of the East.

But soon they began to see small bands of Indians at a distance and Joseph Milner demanded that his daughter ride close to the wagons. She was sorry to give up the pleasure of scampering about away from the caravan. Then one day a band of several hundred Indians in war paint suddenly appeared around the wagons. Young Joe caught up with his sister as she rode along on her burro. "There's no women or children in that bunch," he said with a frown. "That's not a good sign."

When the train stopped for the noon meal, the Indians rode boldly up to the wagons, dismounted and came into the camp. This was the first that Sarah had seen of an Indian so close. She stared with wide and frightened, but fascinated eyes as the Indians impudently put their hands into the men's pockets in search of tobacco or pocket knives. They scooped bacon out of the frying pans to eat as soon as it was cooked. Sarah looked at her father for a sign of what would happen next. "Starting trouble over such little things," he said to her, "is foolish. God grant us the strength to endure this indignity with the best grace we can."

After lunch, Sarah was riding her burro close to her parents wagon when an old chief pulled up next to her. He rode so close that he crowded Sarah against the wagon. She stayed as close to her father as she could. Finally the chief came so close to her that he reached across and twirled his dirty finger into one of her curls. Sarah's mother still arranged her hair for her each morning. Sarah gave a cry of alarm. Joseph Milner jumped from the wagon and helped his daughter up onto the wagon, then jumped back up onto the seat next to her. The Indians found this to be highly amusing and they all cackled like evil crows. Sarah had been terrified by the incident and for years afterward would have dreams of the Indian's hot breath on her neck, and she would awaken with a shudder.

The wagon train was now approaching Julesburg. Word had been passed down the line to keep moving as fast as possible so as to reach the encampment and relative safety by nightfall. After the noon meal, the Milner party took the lead in the wagon train and trudged on. During the afternoon heavy, black clouds began to form and spread across the vast expanse of the horizon. The animals began to be restive and unmanageable. Suddenly the cows at the lead of the teams bolted on a long downslope and the oxen dashed after them. The second wagon bolted as well and began a headlong flight down the long hill, scattering the possessions of the family everywhere out the back of the wagons. By the time the family had brought the animals under control and gathered up all their supplies, the lumbering wagon train had passed them by and was now out of sight over the horizon. The family was alone in the heart of hostile country, and now it had started to rain.

Grimly the Milner family tried to catch up with the other wagons as the lightning flashed and the rain came down in torrents, but by sundown they had not gained any ground and their animals were exhausted and refused to be driven another step. They had no choice but to pull up at the base of a slope and make camp for the night. The animals were closely herded to the wagons. A hot meal was prepared and that made everyone feel better. The storm had subsided to a drizzle and they all feel into a troubled sleep, worn out by the excitement and exertions of the day.

The following morning, Joseph Milner was anxious to get his family out of the open and into the protection of the larger group of wagons. Sarah was desperately afraid that the Indians would find them all alone out here, and they would be killed. Soon the oxen were placed in their yokes and the wagons rolled briskly to the west. Within a hour they spotted the smoke from the big encampment at Julesburg and before noon the family jogged into the comfort of the large numbers of people who were already there.

There was great excitement in the camp at Julesburg as Sarah and her family rode in. Scouts had been out since first light and now they returned to say that a small trading post just a few miles away had been raided during the night and that the lone trader, who had lived among the Indians for years had been killed and scalped. His store had been looted.

"Does this mean that the Indians may attack us?" asked Sarah of one of the scouts.

"Could be, Miss," said the scout. "Something sure has 'em stirred up."

The Milner family took their assigned place in the big camp. All of the wagons were drawn into a huge circle. The oxen and cattle were placed in a close herd near the wagons to graze and an armed guard was set to watch them during the night. A common tactic for the Indians was to rush in under the cover of darkness and stampede the stock. In case of any attack, the emigrants would drive the stock into the space between the wagons. The long night passed without any appearance of the Indians.

With the rising sun, calmness was restored in the camp. A detail of soldiers arrived from the Julesburg station and finding that the required number of 100 wagons had now arrived, gave permission for the settlers, emigrants, and freight wagons to proceed toward Denver and the other destinations along the Front Range.

Sarah, all thoughts of being an invalid now just a memory left behind in the East, strode along with the wagons in a picture of robust good health. She looked across the wide plains and was moved by the impressive sight of all those wagons strung out single file in the bright Colorado sunshine. They were now at last within the borders of Colorado Territory, and Sarah began to look forward to the end of their journey.

Within just a few days of travel along the South Platte river, the great snow-capped peaks of the Rocky Mountains began to grow on the horizon. "Look, Papa," she cried in her excitement, "I never thought I should see such a sight as this. I shall never forget this moment or that glorious skyline!"

Now the leisurely pace that the family had taken through all these months was abandoned as the great wagon train rolled on, spurred ahead relentlessly by the wagons of the freight companies who were anxious to deliver their loads in Denver and the mining camps and begin their return journey to the Missouri River.

On the 4th of July, 1864, exactly 12 weeks from the day they had left Rockford, Illinois, Sarah Milner and her family arrived on the banks of Cherry Creek. The long journey was over. The river was still running high and muddy from a flood that had occurred nearly a month before. Sarah heard talk in the wagon camp of a much bigger flood that had washed down a river called the Cache La Poudre during the same storm and had destroyed an entire army camp at a place, further north, called Laporte.

Men, women and families who had been strangers a few weeks before, now gathered together in the fading light of day around their campfires, as the last of the sunset burned the tops of the great mountains in frightful orange.

Several men who had been here in the wilderness for many years stopped by the Milner camp for hot coffee and some of the fresh bread that had been baked just that afternoon. "Well," said one of them, "How do you like it here, so far?" Sarah looked up from her coffee gazed at across the horizon. "Its beautiful and strange. Like nothing I've ever seen before."

"Before you've been out here very long, you'll have seen many strange things." The others nodded their heads in agreement. "The first thing you need to cultivate is an open mind to any possibility, because *anything* is possible out here. You abandoned the word impossible back in Illinois when you left."

None disputed this great truth.

One by one, the old-timers and the newcomers alike drifted away to sleep. The aroma of the dying fire faded as the smoke drifted away into the trees. No one was left to breath the crisp, fresh air of the night except Sarah. She sat quietly and looked at the stars.

The pioneers brought all their hopes and dreams to the frontier. They came to build a new way of life and ended up building a country. It was never easy. William, the oldest son never made it to Colorado. He died on the family's trek west.

The Milner family did not settle immediately in the Poudre Valley. First they went to the gold camps near Central City, and also they spent time in southern Colorado. Eventually they settled for good along the Big Thompson near present day Loveland. Several members of the family made real contributions and Milner Mountain, Milner Creek and Milner Pass, at the west end of Trail Ridge Road, are all named for the family.

Sarah Ann Milner married Edward Smith. She and her husband homesteaded in the Poudre Valley. In 1868, Sarah became the first school teacher in Larimer County at the first school. The doctor who predicted that Sarah Ann would not survive even the journey across the plains never knew how wrong he was. She died in 1939 at the age of 95.

The 1864 Flood Of The Poudre River.

On the same day that the Milner family was cut off from their wagon train on the prairie just outside of Julesberg and were huddled alone in the midst of a great storm, the same storm had been raining all day at Camp Collins, the army camp just west of Laporte. The winter had been just miserable with more snow than even the Indians could remember. Now the spring had been hot, and the Poudre River had been flowing nearly bank high for almost a month. It was early June, the 9th, in 1964. Captain William Evans, commander of the two companies of the 11th Ohio Cavalry at Camp Collins, gazed with worried eyes the skies to the West. He had good reason to be worried.

The storm in Laporte was nothing compared to what was happening in the mountains to the west. A monster of a thunderstorm was hanging over the upper watershed of the Poudre River, and the torrents of rain were melting the huge snowpack that had been accumulating all winter. Swiftly the entire torrent of water began to sweep down the canyon in a raging flood

Through the night, the flood grew and the water flowed

faster and faster pushing before it trees, rocks, dirt and animals. The narrow Poudre Canyon itself was filling up like an irrigation ditch and pushing toward the canyon mouth. Camped on the flood plain, right next to the river, were the two companies of the 11th Ohio Cavalry.

In the middle of the night of June 9th, 1864, the crest of the flood of the Poudre River reached the mouth of the canyon. A wall of water 20 feet high burst out of the canyon and the explosion was so loud you could hear it for 15 miles. Released from the bondage of the canyon walls, the flood quickly overflowed the banks of the Poudre River and began to spread out going 30 miles an hour in all directions. The crest of the flood was upon soldiers at Camp Collins before anyone knew what was happening. Tents, clothing, ordinance, stores of food, grain and hay, and the horses and mules, disappeared in the blink of an eye.

The terrified soldiers ran for their lives toward the nearest bluff. Some of the men who were sleeping in cabins found that the water was rising so fast that they couldn't push the doors open against the water. So they went out through the chimneys, huddling on the roofs. Soon the cabins themselves began to fall apart and wash away, so the men had to jump into the water and swim or wade to higher ground, grumbling about the "Nitwit who placed the camp so close to the river." But in the dark, with the rain continuing to fall and the roar of the river so loud that you couldn't hear a man yelling in your ear, there was nothing to do but huddle together for warmth and wait for the terrible night to pass.

The flood of the Poudre River destroyed the entire garrison at Camp Collins. All of the supplies and all of the horses and mules had been swept away. Every building in Laporte had been flooded and the entire population had to flee to higher ground. On the bluffs to the south a wagon train of 200 wagons was stranded until the water receded. When morning broke, Captain William Evans could see that the entire area was completely submerged. The roofs of a few cabins could be seen floating above the water. For as far as the eye could see, there was nothing but one vast lake of muddy water.

In spite of all the damage and destruction that the flood had brought, amazingly, not a single life, that they could determine, had been lost. With the passing of the storm, it would be some time before the water receded off the flood plain and back into the river. Still the Poudre ran bank high and swiftly for the balance of the month. The army had a big job of rebuilding, and it was necessary to do so quickly since the wagon trains and the emigrants would soon began to move once more with the coming of better weather.

"The Army Years"
1864-1867

THE POUDRE VALLEY. *"We, of the present day, call it the beautiful valley, and it is so, with its fine farms, its green fields, its growing cities and beautiful homes, but with the touches of this civilization, it is no more beautiful now, it can never appear as beautiful to anyone as it appeared on those June mornings in 1852, clothed in that garb that Nature placed there."*

Ansel Watrous,
"History of Larimer County"

An artist's drawing of the Fort Collins Military Reservation as it appeared in 1865.

Fort Collins Library

Relocating The Military Garrison

The Poudre Valley was a steaming, swirling cauldron of mud. Morning had dawned to a landscape that looked more like an ocean than a prairie. During the night, the Cache La Poudre River had surged out of its banks and spread for miles in all directions from the foothills east. The soldiers at Camp Collins, just west of Laporte, were huddled in small groups on the high ground around the river bottom. They were wet and cold and miserable. However, they were alive. When the flood had flashed through the camp in the middle of the night, the soldiers had run for their lives. Now as they looked back at their camp, all they could see was the roofs of a few cabins that had not been washed away, sticking out of the water, like a little fleet of boats lost at sea. Everything they had was gone. All their supplies, food, horses and personal possessions had been ripped away in the fury of the storm and flood that had struck them while they slept in the night . . . and filled the valley like a bathtub. It was the morning of June 10th, 1864.

Captain William Evans, commander of the two companies of the 11th Ohio Cavalry, looked darkly at the gloomy sight. His one consolation was that none of his men had been killed in the flood. Everything else was a complete loss. He had heard the grumbling of his men who complained about the "nitwit" who had placed the camp so close to the river. Evans knew that he was the "nitwit". But soldiers had used this sight as a camp for years and never had any trouble. It was just his bad luck that brought his command to the valley of the Cache La Poudre just two weeks before.

Still, some other arrangement would have to be made now. Not only was Evans going to have to find a new sight for a military camp that was safe from the rampages of the river, but he also was going to need land that was not claimed by civilians who had homesteaded the Poudre Valley.

In the next several weeks, Evans was busy getting his command back into some semblance of order. New supplies, provisions and livestock had to be brought south from the big military base at Fort Laramie. The Overland Stage line had to be reestablished and service restored. The army lent whatever assistance it could to the settlers in Laporte, and the wagon trains that were eager to move on to their destinations. Plus patrols had to be mounted to keep watch over the territory and protect it from the many war parties of Indians that were moving across the land. The Poudre River continued to flow fast and bank high throughout the entire month of June and was difficult to cross.

Finally, in July of 1864, Colonel William Collins, the commander of the garrison at Fort Laramie, ordered Captain Evans to look for a new site for a military camp further down river and in a more favorable location. The man who got the job was Lieutenant Jim Hannah and he led a small detail of soldiers out of Laporte to survey the land and report his recommendation for a better site. Lt. Hannah came down the Poudre as far east as I-25 is today. Then he crossed the river and started back upstream on the south bank. He reached a farm, located at about the intersection of today's College Avenue and the river. The farm was owned by a man named Joseph Mason.

"First" Citizen Of The Valley.

People who have the ability to create civilization from a wilderness, a city out of a prairie are rare indeed. If they are highly colorful to boot, then you have a real unique person on your hands. That's the kind of man that Joseph Mason was. In all my studies of our history, Joseph Mason seems to me to be the one indispensable man without whom it is unlikely that history would have turned out as it did. At every critical point in the development of first the fort and then the city in its early years, you will find Joseph Mason left his mark. Colonel William O. Collins may be our namesake, but Joseph Mason should probably be considered the Father of the City. Indeed, of all the others, Joseph Mason had the clearest Vision of all, along the Poudre Valley.

Mason was born on January 28, 1840 in Montreal, Canada. He attended school in Montreal and received a fair education. He left home when he was just 15 years old . . . out to seek his fortune, so to speak. He spent the next four years drifting south and west. By the time he was

The only known likeness of Joseph Mason, the man most responsible for the establishment of Fort Collins, the army post and city. He was Larimer County Commissioner at the age of 22. He was also the county's largest businessman during the army years and through the establishment of the city of Fort Collins.   Fort Collins Library

19 years old he had arrived in the Rocky Mountains with a government expedition that was exploring the headwaters of the Yellowstone River. He left the party at its winter camp and struck out, by himself, in the dead of winter. It was sort of a reconnaissance by one of a huge wilderness, but then Joseph Mason was a brave man. He arrived at Laporte on February 10, 1860 where he found a settlement of mountaineers and trappers, 50 or 60 strong and four or five hundred Indians. In terms of the famous people who would be the true builders of Fort Collins, Joseph Mason was the first to arrive.

Mason is not a famous forefather of the Fort just because he got here first. When he first saw the valley it was the winter of 1860. Mason liked what he saw. His education told him that the Poudre Valley was a tremendously valuable piece of real estate. He could see that very soon, a lot of people would be coming here to live . . . People who would need things . . . People who were willing to pay for what he had. The only problem just then was that he didn't have anything, nor did he have the money to buy it. So he took off to see if he couldn't make a little money.

For the next two years, Mason moved around through the mining camps all over Colorado. We don't know much about what he did during this time, but in 1862, he showed up again in the Poudre Valley with money in his pocket, and he made his first investment in real estate. He bought a farm on the river, along today's College Avenue and just north of the old power plant. Then he settled in and became the first real resident of Fort Collins. In 1862, when Larimer County was formed by the Territorial Legislature, Mason was picked by Governor Evans to be one of the three county commissioners with Laporte as the county seat. So the very first government to ever come to our part of the country was presided over by this man.

Well, when Lt. Jim Hannah got to Mason's farm, he was eager to get the advise of this important Poudre Valley veteran. Joe Mason was eager to give some advice. He had Lt. Hannah climb down off his horse and a bottle of whiskey appeared. The good lieutenant was certainly not one to argue with such a well informed and . . . generous man, so there they sat, in the new grass of summer, along the banks of a fast-flowing Poudre River, while Joe Mason waxed poetic about what a wonderful place this would be to build a army post . . . and refilling Lt. Hannah's glass, often. Mason pointed out that this was land that was claimed by no one, except for prairie dogs, and afforded an excellent view of the surrounding land. Well, there was *one* settler . . . Mason himself, but he didn't actually own any land on the proposed military reservation. He owned a bunch of land *around* the new military reservation. How convenient. That it had also escaped the ravages of the flood the previous month was obvious. Furthermore, in his capacity as county commissioner, Joseph Mason was in a wonderful position to do the army a lot of good.

For whatever reason, logic or liquor, Lt. Hannah did, in fact, write a report that recommended the site pointed out by Joseph Mason. This report was forwarded to Colonel Collins at Fort Laramie.

A Picture Of "Fort Collins".

On August 13th, 1864, Colonel William Collins arrived with his guard of soldiers in the Poudre Valley to look over the site that had been picked by Lt. Hannah. He stayed in the area for over a week, checking and evaluating the site. Then on August 21st, he wrote out Special Order Number One that directed that a new military camp be established. He stood near the corner of today's Jefferson and Linden streets and sketched out his plan for a military reservation. He directed that the land be surveyed from the river, south to about today's Prospect Street, and east and west from about Shields Street to Lemay. This made the military post over 6,000 acres in size. Colonel Collins also sketched out detailed plans for the post itself with a parade grounds that were surrounded by barracks, officers quarters, headquarters building, commissary, infirmary, stables and supply buildings that were located from Jefferson Street to the river. August 21, 1864, becomes the birthday of Fort Collins, Colorado Territory. It was named for Colonel Collins, and the order was approved by President Abraham Lincoln on November 14th.

First of all, we need to get a better picture of what the military fort actually looked like. If you are conjuring up images of

An actual, rare photograph of Fort Collins in 1864. The parade ground with a flag pole is in the foreground. On the left is Old Grout, the officer's quarters are in the center and the headquarters building is on the right.   Fort Collins Library

a big fort with a stockade and guard towers on the corners . . . forget it. It was nothing at all like that. Those kinds of forts are more Hollywood than history. Actually, Fort Collins was laid out in a way that was standard within the military. The post was built around a parade ground that was 300 feet square. The four closest landmarks from today would be a square starting at the corner of Jefferson and Linden Streets, going west to the old Union Pacific station that is now the Jefferson Station Restaurant, north to the Aztlan Center, east to the El Burrito Restaurant, and then south back to the corner of Linden and Jefferson. Everything was built around that square. The headquarters building and the officer's quarters were on the south side of the square. That puts them along Jefferson Street, facing the river. The enlisted men's barracks were on the east side of the parade ground. The stables and corrals for the horses and other stock were on the west and north side, along the river. When the fort really got going a year later, there would be a total of 22 buildings in the fort complex . . . but not a single wall.

In setting up a military post, the army would contract out certain services to civilians. These included some sort of special arrangements for lodging and feeding the officers, and a store from which everybody bought whatever they needed, sort of like the "7/11 of the West." The civilian, called The Sutler, paid a commission to the army for the privilege of the monopoly, but was free to make all the money he could beyond that. Guess who showed up to apply for the Sutler's position? Why it was none other than widely-known, well-respected Joseph Mason, the 24-year-old Larimer County Commissioner. You remember him? He's the fellow who owned the big farm on the other side of the river. He's the fellow who recommended this site for the fort in the first place . . . Well, after giving it some thought, the army selected Joseph Mason as the Post Sutler at Fort Collins. Smart people, those settlers.

Another pretty smart person is an entirely different story. Suddenly arriving on the scene is the venerable Elizabeth Hickok Robbins Stone. She sticks out like an elephant in a herd of field mice. A white women . . . in the Poudre Valley . . . in 1864??!!! Unheard of! In fact, she was the only one! Not only that, but she was also 63 years old. She immediately became "Auntie" Stone to everyone as she built a little boarding house for the officers of Fort Collins. She built her two story cabin across the road and near the corner of Jefferson and Linden. Joseph Mason's store was on the other corner. These two strong settlers become citizens one and two of today's Fort Collins. Of all of the structures built during the years of the active fort, the only building that remains is Auntie Stone's cabin, now preserved at the Fort Collins Museum.

The Grand Dame Of The West.

Elizabeth Stone's life spanned nearly the entire 19th century. She was born in 1801 in Connecticut. By 1829, she and her husband moved to St. Louis, the flourishing center of the western fur trade. At age 51 her first husband died, leaving her with eight children. During the 1850s, she married Lewis Stone, and the whole family moved to Minnesota.

Then, in 1864, she and her husband heard that the army in the West was planning to build a new fort along the banks of a river called the Cache La Poudre in the Colorado Territory. The whole family packed up and moved lock, stock and barrel to Colorado and asked for and received permission to build a cabin on the grounds of the new Fort Collins to serve as a boarding house and mess hall for the officers of the fort. The cabin was a two-story structure that was built near the corner of today's Jefferson and Linden.

The remarkable Elizabeth Hickok Robbins Stone (Auntie Stone). She died in Fort Collins in 1895 at the age of 94.   Fort Collins Library

Elizabeth ran her boarding house, cooked for the officers and was loved and admired by everybody. She had a friendly, happy disposition and was known by everyone as "Auntie". In 1866, Lewis Stone died. This was the second time that Auntie

Stone had been widowed, but she went on in the tradition of the West and kept right on cooking for the officers at the fort and caring for her children and growing number of grandchildren. She even started a new business.

In partnership with Henry Clay Petersen, the gunsmith at Fort Collins, Auntie Stone built a flour mill for the Poudre Valley. The 65-year-old widow seemed to have a practical sense of just what was needed in the development of a community. A flour mill was an important first step in that process. The mill is regarded as the first commercial business in Fort Collins and it flourished. It continues even today, under the name of Ranchway Feeds. The original stone foundations and much of the original construction is still there, along the river, near the Lincoln Street bridge.

Even though the army pulled out of Fort Collins in 1867, Auntie Stone remained and continued to be a part of the history of the Poudre Valley for years and years.

"Fort Collins" Goes To Work.

Prior to the establishment of Fort Collins in 1864, during the Civil War from 1861 to 1864, most of the regular army troops were withdrawn from the frontier for more serious fighting in the East. The Indians seized on this opportunity to declare a war of their own.

From their point of view, their entire way of life and, indeed their very existence, was being threatened. They were faced with a never-ending flood of emigrants pouring into their ancestral homes. They had seen their lands stolen, their food supply slaughtered and their people indiscriminately killed. From the white man's point of view, the Indians were simply a sub-human, aboriginal race to be swatted aside, like so many flies, in their "manifest destiny" to occupy and dominate the entire continent. The Native Americans could not be permitted to establish independent nations within the limits of the continent.

So the government proceeded to regard all Indians as a part of the country, but not worthy of citizenship or it rights and privileges. Very soon the Indians learned that the white men were perfectly serious in their bargaining position, which was, "Give us what we want, or we will beat the Hell out of you and take it anyway."

Furthermore, the white man also said, "We want you all to

become like us and live like we do." Somewhat understandably the Indians said, "NO! We aren't going to do that!" And the fight was on.

At any rate, by the time that the post was established at Fort Collins in 1864, the Indians had been at war for three years and the situation in Colorado was serious, indeed.

This was why a military fort was put in the Poudre Valley in the first place — to provide a centralized strong point, north and south, along the Cherokee Trail and the Overland Stage line that ran along the Front Range of the Rockies from Denver to Fort Laramie, and north of present day Cheyenne. The towns of Cheyenne and Laramie did not exist in 1864. The job of the military was to protect the lives and property of all settlers in the area. And they needed all the help they could get.

When Colonel Collins had signed the order creating the Fort in the summer of 1864, Captain William Evans, who would be in command at Fort Collins, did not waste any time in getting his headquarters moved, the buildings built, and a quick routine established. Sioux, Cheyenne and some Arapaho war parties were marauding all over the plains and there was no way of knowing when they might make a raid into Colorado . . . and the Poudre Valley.

Early borders at Auntie Stone's boarding house in this 1866 photo, celebrating the first Fort Collins Christmas.

Fort Collins Library

The post at Fort Collins was built to accommodate two companies of soldiers, about 150 men. This command of soldiers were expected to ride shotgun over about 15,000 square miles, basically all of northern Colorado clear to the Wyoming line. They were a little short-handed!! Even worse, at any given time the Indians could put ten times that number in the field. At least the soldiers here were regular army, the 11th Ohio Cavalry.

Of course the odds of the whole command actually being *at* Fort Collins at one time were very remote. Most of the time the soldiers were scattered all over creation on a variety of jobs.

They rode escort for the stages, some of them were assigned to the stations themselves at Livermore and Virginia Dale. Part of them were busy chopping down the forest we used to have on the ridge along Horsetooth Reservoir, so they would have wood for the new buildings. And there was always the odd dignitary, congressman or high ranking officer to be escorted about. They had a pretty hard life, and there were some desertions. But for the most part, the soldiers did their jobs as well as they could.

Nevertheless, Captain Evans was congratulating himself. He had gotten the camp moved, quarters built, and the command settled before winter. And with the coming of winter, he could look forward to several months of relative peace from the Indians. Unfortunately, other events in the Colorado Territory would upset the quiet winter scene.

In November of 1864 something happened that would set the stage for the events that occurred in the Poudre Valley for the next two years. A man named John Chivington assembled all the army troops he could get his hands on in the Colorado Territory and proceeded to march out to put a stop to all these Indian threats, once and for all. He found a camp of Cheyenne and Arapaho in eastern Colorado at Sand Creek. The Indians were actually coming in to surrender, but Chivington paid no attention to that. He also paid no attention to the fact that the camp of between 500 and 1000 Indians was filled with mostly women, children and old men. It was wintertime and most of the men were out hunting. Nevertheless, Chivington sent his forces to attack the peaceful Indians asleep in their teepees. Chivington killed them all. He massacred the camp right down to the children and infants. Even at a time when killing Indians was perfectly acceptable, this was regarded by many as an atrocity.

There was absolutely no doubt in the Indian's minds what it was — it was murder, and the white man was going to pay! In spite of the fact that it was the worst part of the winter, food was scarce and it was very dangerous to move around on the open plains in this weather, the Cheyenne, Arapaho and much of Sioux Indian nations took to the warpath south, along the South Platte River, toward Denver.

This was no little raiding party of Indians. The Cheyenne, Arapaho and Sioux were enraged at the slaughter of their people. Some say that as many as 2,000 warriors were in the force that crossed into Colorado Territory in early January, 1865. At Julesburg they wiped out an entire wagon train and simultaneously cut the stage line at the Valley and Junction stations along the South Platte. They attacked homesteads, sacked and burned the buildings, killed all the men and took the women and children captive. The Indians were mostly unopposed, except by some desperate settlers who were getting wiped out at their front doors. The speed at which the party was moving was incredible. The Indians were probing at eight places along a 100 mile front. On the 15th of January, the Indians struck at three ranches between today's Fort Morgan and Sterling. All of the ranches were burned and many were killed. The survivors became refugees headed for Fort Collins.

Fort Collins was not in much better shape. The Chivington massacre at Sand Creek had taken many soldiers from the command, so in January of 1865 the entire Poudre Valley was protected by no more than 60 men. Chivington himself had been relieved following Sand Creek, and the new commander of the Colorado Volunteers was Colonel Thomas Moonlight. He had taken over just three days before the Indian uprising. Moonlight discovered that he had inherited a command with no troops, no horses and no weapons. Moonlight reported back to his general in Kansas that he only had a total of 200 men to protect the entire Front Range.

Winterkill

The news of the Indian attacks in northern Colorado were greeted by Colonel William Collins, commander of the post at Fort Laramie, with great alarm. Realizing that unless reinforcements were sent and soon, it was possible that the entire population of the Poudre Valley might be slaughtered by the rampaging Indians. So, he detailed Lt. Jim Hannah to hurry to Fort Collins with Company L of the 11th Ohio Cavalry to bolster Captain Evans tiny force. Hannah was the man who had scouted the location for the new Fort Collins the previous year. On January 18th, Hannah led his company of 70 men and horses south to the Poudre Valley. The story of that march is one of the great tales of our history.

The 100-mile trek from Fort Laramie to Fort Collins by Lt. Jim Hannah's company of soldiers started off all right on a sunny day. But the next morning, the troop awakened to a foot of snow and a driving blizzard with plummeting temperatures. Throughout the whole day the storm raged on. There was not a single house between the two forts in which to take refuge. That night, the boys from Ohio, some of them from the best families in the state, tasted the first bitterness of their terrible march. That night they made camp as best they could. Very few of them slept as the snow continued to fall along with the temperature. When morning came, they began plodding on, knowing that to fall behind in this trackless wilderness would mean certain death.

Lt. Jim Hannah is standing on the far, upper left, with other officers at Fort Laramie in 1864. Caspar Collins, son of Lt. Col. William O. Collins and the man for who Casper, Wyoming is named standing below, 2nd from right. Fort Collins Library

Hannah was supposed to be taking his troop to reinforce the garrison at Fort Collins against the Indians. Now, he and his troop were fighting for their lives against an enemy that was just as deadly — the weather. By the end of the third day's march, the soldiers and the horses were becoming frozen and barely able to proceed. Finally, at about 4 p.m. in the afternoon, Hannah ordered the company to stop and make camp for the night. It was now snowing harder than ever.

"That night was a night of horrors," one of the troopers wrote in his journal. They had made camp as best they could in a small depression in the apparently limitless plains. The two wagons were set up against the howling wind. The men piled up all their saddles and laid their buffalo robes on the snow. They found a little wood nearby and made enough fire for a few to heat some coffee. The horses were fed and then turned their tails to the wind and lay down in the snow. In only a short while, snow had drifted over them all, till all you could see were heads sticking out of the snow. With that, Hannah's company of men settled down to spend a very long, long night.

The men of the 11th Ohio Cavalry struggle in the blizzard to survive and reach Fort Collins to reinforce the garrison.

Fort Collins Library

On the morning of January 22, 1865, the company was 50 miles north of Fort Collins. The only sign of life that came with the dawn were the snow-covered heads of the horses and little jets of steam coming from under the blankets and buffalo robes. Slowly the men began to move around. The horses were fed again. The men ate hard bread and frozen bacon. They could not get a fire started and so the day's march began. The younger men were freezing to death in their saddles. Jim Hannah went up and down the line screaming at his men to stay awake and keep moving. Somehow, the day passed and as night once again approached, the half dead soldiers seemed to settle down in a state of lethargic dispair: horses exhausted, the men were cold — chilled to the bone. There was no wood, no shelter from the piercing blizzard, the mercury was down to 30 below zero. The troop was stuck on the ridge near today's Cheyenne. And there was nothing ahead but another long, cheerless night in the storm that seemed to never let up. Many of the men had frozen feet. Few were *not* frostbitten. The horses seemed lifeless. Death stared the boys of the Ohio Cavalry in the face. Night fell. The storm went on.

Many of the soldiers had given up hope. They had been out in this blizzard for three days, and the cold winds of the night were slowly sucking the life from them. But Jim Hannah was not finished. In the middle of the night he went from man to man, rousting them from their lethargy. He set the soldiers to unloading all the supplies from the wagons and stacking them up for a windbreak. Then he had the wagons chopped into firewood. By clustering together and keeping out of the wind, they succeeded in getting a fire started.

"Oh what joy! What hope! What cheer," wrote a soldier in his journal, "that a fire with its heat and light can give." They were able to make some hot, strong, fragrant coffee, the first in two days and nights. Over a dozen of the men were crippled and helpless from frozen hands and feet. Their comrades laid them side by side and banked them with snow to keep them warm. Two fires were built and for a while warmth brought life back into the men. Some of them saw their socks burned off their feet without feeling the pain of the fire, so cold were they and so numb were their hands and feet. But soon the wind came up again and blew the fires to pieces and scattered every ember. The dark night closed in again. The strength of the soldiers was nearly gone.

When the morning of January 23rd finally dawned, the storm had blown itself out. The day itself dawned to a deep, electric blue sky and the sun shone, even though it was still 30 degrees below zero. More than half the command was frostbitten and unable to walk. More than half the horses were either dead or too weak to carry a rider. Lt. Hannah had the men lighten their loads as much as possible. All their supplies, arms and saddles were stacked in the snow and abandoned. They must reach Fort Collins today or they would all surely die. The last march began.

To stop again meant death for all, so the soldiers and their horses plodded through the snow and the big drifts the whole morning. At last they came upon the Poudre River, just a few miles above Fort Collins, and they knew that they would survive. Shortly before noon, the company limped into the fort. Never did the beautiful valley appear more glorious and fascinating than on that January morning. None of them would ever forget their ordeal, however most of the men did recover and saw action against the Indians that summer. Before the march of the 11th Ohio soldiers in the blizzard, the situation on the plains had continued to grow worse. No matter what, the company of 70 soldiers of regular army were welcome reinforcements for Fort Collins as the Indian offensive continued.

Lt. Jim Hannah continued with the army for a few years and then resigned his commission to take up a civilian life in the territory. He went on to be a successful settler and businessman. In 1891, he became the Speaker of the House of Representatives in the Colorado General Assembly.

The Poudre Valley Is Mobilized.

Even with the addition of the extra troops Colonel Thomas Moonlight, the commander of the Colorado Cavalry, was desperate. He had a full scale Indian uprising on his hands and too few troops to meet the challenge. He appealed to the territorial governor, Samuel Elbert to call out the militia, which he did, but nobody showed up after they found out that there was no money to pay them. Moonlight pressed the legislature to pass a bill to pay salaries and buy horses, but the legislature debated the issue for days. Meanwhile, the Indians were a formidable force that was wreaking havoc in northern Colorado. The climax of this offensive came on February 2, 1865, when Julesburg was attacked and burned and the telegraph cables were stripped. This meant that Colorado was cut off. That was the last straw for Moonlight, and he resorted to drastic measures to raise a militia. On February 6th, he declared martial law and shut down every business in Denver until he had raised six companies of men. But that didn't solve his problem.

Captain William Evans, commander at Fort Collins, is in the center with the large hat. He is standing in front of the headquarters building in 1864. He was quite unpopular with the settlers, because he was so pompous.   Fort Collins Library

Now he had to find horses for all these troops and they were even more scarce than soldiers. Moonlight sent a letter to Captain William Evans in Fort Collins looking for help. Evans responded by broadcasting an order for a general mobilization of the Poudre Valley. He ordered every man between the ages of 18 and 50 to convene in Fort Collins on February 11th. Since 18 to 50 years old included just about the entire population of the valley, just about everyone showed up, even though Captain Evans was certainly not one of their favorite people. On the appointed day, the fort was crowded with people to hear Evans speech. The pompous captain mounted a whiskey barrel a began to speak.

"DENIZENS OF THE WILDERNESS!" he began. "War is breaking out in all directions, and the peace of the valley is being threatened! I hereby declare martial law and I will hold you all FIRMLY as I would a wine glass in the hollow of my hand! Even now, my troops are under fire at Fremont's Orchard! I call you to arms as reserve militia to cooperate with my warriors in suppressing these ruthless invaders . . . and if any man does not obey my commands, I will make wolf bait of his carcass, BY GOD, SIR!"

As it turned out, the mobilization of the Poudre Valley was unnecessary, at least for the time being. The sack of Julesburg was the last of the raids on northern Colorado for that winter. The Cheyenne and Sioux had moved back to the Black Hills to continue their raids there. In the midst of all this, Chief Friday and his 250 Arapaho had been quietly wintering not far from Fort Collins. Friday's influence had kept them out of the battles and out of trouble. The settlers viewed them suspiciously, but nevertheless as noncombatants.

The Indians Of The Poudre Valley.

Just about all of the conflicts with the Indians in the Poudre Valley came from outside the valley. However, an entire tribe of Arapaho lived in the valley and continued to live here through the Indian wars, and they truly were noncombatants. In fact, our Arapaho regarded the settlers as a giant supermarket or, at least, as an industry. Now this didn't just happen. A lot of the character in the relationship between the local Arapaho and the white man was fashioned by a single man. His name was Friday Fitzpatrick. He was the leader of the several hundred Arapaho who lived in the Poudre Valley. Not only was he quite intelligent, but he had seen with his own eyes the power of the people who were bearing down on him and on his way of life. Very early on, he decided that he would negotiate for the best deal possible from the settlers in hopes of preserving something. Since you probably have never seen an Arapaho Indian around here, you can assume he was not successful. But the story is worth telling.

In 1831, the famous mountain man and scout Thomas Fitzpatrick was trapping along the front range when he came across a little six year old Indian boy who had been lost from his tribe and orphaned. Just

Chief Friday Fitzpatrick. Raised and educated in a Catholic school, he spoke perfect English and was the leader of the Poudre Valley Arapaho.

as in the story of <u>Robinson Crusoe</u>, Fitzpatrick found the boy on Friday and so that's what he called the young Indian. He also did something else very important. He took Friday back to St. Louis and put him in a Catholic school. In this way Friday got a decent education, learned to speak excellent English and gained an appreciation of the ways of the white man.

Friday Fitzpatrick was a bright boy. He became an educated, literate, worldly-wise Native American. Fitzpatrick took him to Washington, D.C. in 1851 when he visited with the President of the United States, Millard Fillmore. In Hollywood terms, his visit with the "Great White Father" in Washington, made Friday a very important person among his native Arapaho tribe, and he became chief of the several hundred Indians who lived in the Poudre Valley. Since stories of the savageness of Indians were quite common throughout the frontier, you can just imagine how shocked the early settlers must

Part II: "The Army Years" 1864-1867

have been in the 1860s when the first Indian they saw, came sauntering up and in concise English inquired how business was in St. Louis.

Chief Friday Fitzpatrick presided over his tribe of Arapaho in the Poudre Valley. He had a tremendous advantage in perspective since he was educated and understood things like money, private property, banking and so forth. He told his tribe that if they would be good neighbors to the settlers, offer to help them hunt, and not steal their horses, that they could earn money from the white man for things to make a better life. Well the Arapaho weren't stupid, so that's what they did.

The big problem to Friday's plan of peaceful CO-existence with his Indians and the Poudre Valley settlers was that a lot of new settlers were arriving all the time, and all of them believed that the land was theirs for the taking. The government said so. The papers said so. And Indian relations in the rest of Colorado could not have been worse. But Friday was speaking the truth when he told his people that they could not win, and he did everything he could to stay out of the fighting and on the good side of the settlers in the valley.

By 1864, Friday Fitzpatrick had been forced to accept a treaty that severely limited the Arapaho hunting grounds to a small area in southeastern Colorado. Actually he only went there for a short period of time and then returned to the Poudre Valley. If he had not returned and stubbornly refused to leave, his entire tribe of Arapaho would have been part of the hundreds who were massacred at Sand Creek.

Nevertheless he still had to get permission from the commander at the fort to hunt for food along the river to feed his hungry band of several hundred Arapaho, but he continued to maintain friendly relations with all the settlers. To their credit, there was a large number of people at Fort Collins who abhorred the senseless slaughter of helpless women and children at Sand Creek. After all, they had never had any trouble with Chief Friday's Arapaho.

When the fort was closed in 1867, the Arapaho's plight became almost desperate. They were hungry, and they were sick. Their numbers had now decreased to just a couple hundred. Friday wrote to the governor and was given some food and supplies. Finally, in 1868, Friday learned that chief Washakie of the Shoshone had worked out a settlement for the big Wind River Reservation in Wyoming near Lander. He wrote to Washakie and asked if he could move his Arapaho to the new reservation. Washakie didn't want the Arapaho, but nevertheless Friday and his band showed up in 1869. Even though the tribes had been traditional enemies, Friday chose survival over blood feuds and the Arapaho left the Poudre Valley forever.

Unfortunately, the suffering for the Arapaho continued. White men viewed the hunting and killing of Indians as some sort of holy mission — or at least great sport. One of the original settlers of the Poudre Valley, A.H. Patterson was among a mob of miners and others who went to Lander, Wyoming in 1870, specifically to attack the homeless Arapaho. This is exactly what Patterson, one of our founders, wrote in his diary.

"We expected to surprise the Arapaho camp, but they were on the lookout and we could not get them all. We did get 25 Indians and 14 ponies. We came close to getting old Friday himself, and we did kill four of his Indians. I got one scalp and it is a fine one, you bet. They fought some, but only one of our men were hurt." Pretty sad. The man who was educated in St. Louis, visitor to the President of the United States and who tried everything he could think of to find a way to live with the white man, was reduced to this.

The people who had lived in and cherished this land for untold generations were now gone. What remained of Chief Friday's Arapaho were absorbed into the Wind River Reservation. Friday himself scouted for General Crook during the Indian campaigns of 1876, the same one that included the Battle of the Little Big Horn. He died at the age of 61 in 1881.

It was Friday's leadership that made the relationship of his Arapaho with the settlers of Fort Collins so peaceful. But, in the end, the Arapaho Indians of the Poudre Valley were driven from their hunting grounds, reduced to begging for food, cheated by unscrupulous Indian agents and decimated by sickness, starvation and random killing. By 1899, all that remained were the stories that the early settlers would tell their children. As far as Fort Collins was concerned, the Arapaho were wiped from the face of the earth and today only a few artifacts are preserved in the Fort Collins museum. But the good news is that the Arapaho tribe endures still. Every year they have a gathering of the tribe in Cheyenne to celebrate their culture and remember.

Part II: "The Army Years" 1864-1867

The Poudre Valley Is Burning!

Now national events were taking center stage, even in the West. On April 9,1865, Robert E. Lee was forced to surrender at Appomattox and the Civil War was over. The nation was ready for a heart-felt thanksgiving. But joy and relief turned to sorrow and mourning when less than a week later, Abraham Lincoln was assassinated in a Washington theater. In the gloom that followed, Coloradoans hardly noticed the regular army reinforcements that were starting to arrive along the Front Range. It had been a quiet spring and maybe the Indians would not return to Colorado that summer. The settlers did not know that the worst of the Indian attacks were yet to come.

Fort Collins would fully justify its existence during the summer of 1865 when the spreading Indian Wars would engulf the entire 200 mile stretch of the Cherokee Trail that ran along the Front Range and into Wyoming. This was a main emigrant route, the road of the Overland Stage and the centers for commerce and business. And located right smack dab in the middle of all this was Fort Collins . . . now manned by less than 100 soldiers, over half of which were on detached duty protecting the stage stations north and east of the fort.

The first news that the Indians had returned with substantial war parties to raid the Poudre Valley came in June, 1865. Schuyler Colfax, the Speaker of the House of Representatives for the U.S. Congress was making an inspection tour of the West. He departed from Denver on the way to Salt Lake City on June 3 and arrived in Fort Collins later that day. Soldiers from the garrison were detailed to escort the important man, safely to Fort Halleck in Wyoming. When they got to the Virginia Dale stage station, they learned that raids had occurred further north on the previously peaceful section of the line. They stayed a day at Virginia Dale, and then scooted out of the territory in a hurry. It was shear luck they were not attacked.

When the settlers had been mobilized in February following the sack of Julesburg, the Indian raids stopped. So everybody went back to their regular lives. With the resumption of the Indian offensive, the Poudre Valley, once again, found itself ill prepared and undermanned. The Indian force was estimated at 1,000 warriors. There were only 40 troopers at Fort Collins. On

June 8, the Cheyenne and Sioux raided Laporte, just 8 miles from Fort Collins, and attacked the homestead of Antoine Janis, the valley's first white settler, and drove off his entire herd of about 40 horses. They also attacked two emigrant wagon trains heading north of Fort Collins and killed many people. Now the main road and stage line all the way to Wyoming were under general attack on a daily basis. The army reacted with alarm to all this and dispatched four companies of cavalry to Fort Collins to reinforce the garrison. The soldiers were then split into smaller detachments and posted at the stage stations or scattered throughout northern Colorado. The Indians just bypassed the strong points and went on raiding.

By the end of June, the army thought that it had solved the problem, and they assured Robert Spotswood, who was chief of the Overland Stage in this area, that the line was now safe. So on June 28, Spotswood started back up the line, north from Denver, to re-stock the line and restore service. The farther north he got, the worse the situation became. He arrived at the Virginia Dale station, north of Fort Collins, just in time to be trapped at the station and besieged by a large Indian force for several days. The head of the station had been shot in the chest with an arrow the day before, and he died as Spotswood was arriving. A running battle went on for several days with the 10 defenders at Virginia Dale outnumbered 20 to 1. With food, ammunition and hope running out for them all, they hatched a desperate plan. The men assembled a crazy contraption out of wagon wheels and stove pipe to make the Indians think that they had a cannon. Apparently it worked because the Indians left without another attack. A day later, Spotswood left Virginia Dale to continue his efforts to reopen the stage line. As he went north, he found dead settlers, burned stations, all the stock gone and all the nearby ranchers, clear to the Wyoming line, fighting for their lives.

By August of 1865, the troops were pouring into Fort Collins. Fourteen companies of General George Custer's 7th Cavalry arrived under the command of Colonel George Briggs. Other regular army elements were also reinforcing the garrison at Fort Collins. But the Indians were moving in their own reinforcements and now had as many as 3,000 warriors within striking distance of the bustling fort.

There was no way of knowing where the Indians would strike next. Certainly they existed in sufficient numbers to stage a major attack on the fort itself. Even though the garrison at Fort Collins was now swollen to over four battalions, most of those soldiers were on patrol, and the fort itself was defended by only a few soldiers and settlers. The stage coaches were unable to operate. It was foolhardy to try and leave the fort and escape because there was nowhere to go. The Indians controlled the territory for a hundred miles in all directions. Little Fort Collins stood alone, isolated, cut off, and outnumbered against an enemy that would kill them all if they could. The battle for the Poudre Valley was underway.

Northern Colorado was now the hot spot of the Indian wars of the West. Battle reports were coming in daily. The soldiers at Fort Collins did not have to go far to get into a fight. The Forks stage station at Livermore was attacked and many were killed. One of the soldiers defending the station was captured by the Indians. Then, in full sight of the helpless people at the station, he was shot full of arrows, scalped, tied to the wheel of a wagon and had bacon stacked up around him. Then the Indians set fire to the bacon and the Cheyenne cheered as the soldier died in screams of agony.

Slowly the noose was being tightened around Fort Collins as the Indian forces crept to within a mile of the garrison. Joseph Mason's ranch was within sight of the fort. On August 11th, Indians snuck into his corrals and ran off his whole herd of horses, about 80 of them, and all his cattle. The Indians got another 80 horses at the ranch of Mariano Modena close to mouth of the Big Thompson canyon. Ranches and homesteads were attacked and burned, settlers were put to the knife and their families taken prisoner. Most of those who escaped ran for their lives to Fort Collins.

But the settlers and the soldiers were fighting back. Mariano Modena had jumped on a mule when his horses were stolen and had pursued the Indians, accompanied only by his wife. Soon others joined him to chase a force of nearly a hundred Indians. A running battle was fought all along the valley where Horsetooth Reservoir is today, and right up to the outskirts of Laporte.

The siege of the Fort continued throughout the month of August. By the first of September, the marauding Sioux and Cheyenne were crisscrossing the valley leaving death and destruction behind wherever they went. On September 3rd, a large body of warriors forded the river at Sherwood station near the intersection of today's I-25 and Prospect Road. They were driving several hundred horses. At 1 a.m. the garrison at Fort Collins was mustered . . . all 14 of them, and set off in pursuit of the Indians. After driving their horses to exhaustion and chasing the war party almost all the way north to present day Cheyenne, they were forced to break off the chase and plodded back to the Fort with only a few stray horses to show for their effort.

Across the parade ground on that hot Summer afternoon, Elizabeth Stone, the 64-year-old widow, who ran the boarding house at the Fort for the officers, stood in front of her house. Her hands wrung the apron she was wearing as she gazed, with worried eyes, the far horizons. Down the river was a cloud of dust, made by the hooves of hundreds of horses. To the south, towards the Big Thompson, was the sound of gunfire, and there was smoke of the bluffs north of Laporte. Around the parade ground of the fort, were little camps of refugees who had fled their homes at the last moment, saving what they could and leaving the rest. As night fell, all could see the fires in the sky as, one by one, their homes were sacked and destroyed. The Poudre Valley was burning.

The Closing Of The Military Reservation.

With the coming of the winter of 1865, the Indian attacks abated. The Cheyenne, Sioux and their many allies withdrew to their home territories further north. Also, the summer campaigns had alarmed the army, and reinforcements continued to arrive at Fort Collins. This meant that the Poudre Valley once again became peaceful. So peaceful, in fact, that the now superbly provisioned and well-built Fort Collins was now entering its final year of existence. Even though 22 buildings had been constructed at the fort, other military centers were viewed as being more important and the army was looking for ways to cut costs and consolidate their forces. The final chapter of the military reservation at Fort Collins was about to begin.

"What do you mean, we don't need an army fort in the Poudre Valley?" was the question that most of the settlers asked. Nearly everyone in the valley had lost something or someone during the terrible summer of 1865. Now the army was saying that Fort Collins was unnecessary and ought to be closed. The settlers, led by Joseph Mason, the post Sutler, protested. They believed that the coming of better weather in the spring of 1866 would mean a resumption of Indian raids. The army told the emigrants that they had the situation under control and that they had nothing to worry about. Actually, this was true. The Poudre Valley had been a good place to send war parties from the Cheyenne and Sioux nations. But now, the Indians were being forced to fight on their home lands in Wyoming and the Dakotas, and had no warriors to spare for raids far away in the south in Colorado Territory. Nevertheless, the people who were living in the Poudre Valley had grave misgivings about their safety and said so in no uncertain terms.

Throughout all of 1866, a bewildering array of army units and different commanders came and went from Fort Collins. There were conflicting reports on what the fate of the fort would be. Throughout the summer, a parade of high ranking officers from Washington were making inspections of the western territories. Finally, in early September, 1866, the commander the of new military division of the Missouri that included Larimer County arrived in Fort Collins. This was the Civil War hero, Lt. General William Tecumseh Sherman. If anyone had expected the tough old general to arrive with a flourish of trumpets and an honor guard of escorting cavalry troopers, they were disappointed. The General actually arrived dressed in his grubbiest uniform, with a half-chewed cigar clenched in his teeth and driving a battered old army ambulance like any mule-skinner. He took one look at Fort Collins now manned by just a few dozen soldiers, and said, in effect, "Let's get this dump closed down!" And so it was that on September 22, 1866, the order came to begin an evacuation of the fort. The active life span of Fort Collins was exactly one year and eleven months.

However, everything did not happen overnight. There were still vast stores of supplies and fodder for the stock stored at the fort. General Sherman had ordered that all of these supplies be removed to other military installations. But the army was slow in getting the order implemented, and through the fall and winter of 1866, all of these supplies seemed to just vanish. In fact, the army would eventually order an investigation of what happened to all their stuff. The settlers of the valley were ponderously unhelpful in providing the army with information about the whereabouts of all these supplies. Very

Visions Along The Poudre Valley

likely, the big piles of hay, lumber, food, and other provisions were too big of a temptation and everyone sort of helped themselves. In the end, the old fort just faded away, leaving only the buildings to stand where just a year before the parade grounds had rumbled to the sound of horses and men going off to war.

In January, 1867, a letter written by Harris Stratton, the postmaster of Fort Collins, to President Andrew Johnson was moving through the government bureaucracy. The letter said that the former military reservation at Fort Collins with its 6,160 acres of land should now be turned over by the army to the Department of the Interior and opened for settlement by civilians. The army agreed with all of this and endorsed the letter approving the transfer. However, the government was to discover that the original order establishing the military fort and signed by Abraham Lincoln in November of 1864, had never been properly recorded. And even though President Johnson signed a simple order on March 15, 1867 that directed that the lands of the reservation be released and all of the buildings at the fort be sold, it was not done because the government determined that the entire transaction that established Fort Collins in the first place was highly irregular and that it would take an act of Congress to release the lands of the Fort Collins for civilian settlement. It was a bureaucratic quagmire that would bog down the further development of Fort Collins as a city for over five years.

This did not mean that the settlers who lived in the Poudre Valley were content to sit around and wait for the government to act. On the contrary, some of the men who would later become the driving forces for the establishment of Fort Collins, the city, were already hard at work.

The time of the military fort and its impact on Larimer County had ended. The Army Years were over. A new age of development and bright new dreams was about to begin. The men, women and their families who had come to the West to realize a better life were of sturdy stock. It would not be easy, but then nothing out here on the frontier ever was.

"Old Town"
1867-1878

P IONEERS . . . *"In these modern times, we have a tendency to glamorize life on the frontier too much. It seems like such an adventure. We are certain that the pioneers were just having the time of their lives. Actually just the opposite was true. Most of the settlers in these times were from established and frequently wealthy families in the East. They didn't come to the Poudre Valley so they could have the pleasure of camping out all their lives and getting killed by a hostile environment, hostile living conditions and hostile Indians. They came out here to get rich and to live their lives freely in the manner that seemed best to them.*

The pioneers had no illusions about how difficult their lives would be. For the most part, they knew what they were walking into. However, most of them regarded all this hardship as just a temporary condition that they could correct with a few years of hard work and a little luck. With the end of the Civil War in 1865, the promise of free land from the government was a powerful incentive to get on the road heading West, and tens of thousands did just that."

Speech, prepared by Phil Walker for the
"Society of Professional Journalists, May, 1995"

"But Joe, There Ain't No Fort Collins!"

Since the government had concluded that the entire transaction regarding the land upon which Fort Collins was built was highly irregular, the Army decided that they had, technically, never really owned the land in the first place. It was necessary for Congress to pass legislation freeing the land. Well Congress didn't move any quicker in 1867 than it does today, so this was the beginning of more than five years of frustration before the land was finally released for homesteading.

However, the settlers, who were rugged individualists and just wanted the government to go away and quit bothering them, proceeded with all speed to try and reproduce out here in the West, similar living conditions to what they used to have in the East.

Foremost in this process of getting organized was the establishment of a government infrastructure of their own. This meant that the county was the place to start. When the territory of Colorado had been parceled into counties in 1861, Larimer County was one of those original divisions. The county had commissioners, a court and they kept records. The seat, or capital of Larimer County was placed in Laporte. In 1861, Laporte was the largest center of commerce and population north of Denver, so Laporte was the obvious choice.

But now it was 1867, and things had changed. For the past three years, Fort Collins, the military fort, had been the principal center of activity in Larimer County. That the fort had been closed down didn't change anything, because the principal business of the valley was being done at Joseph Mason's Sutler store, located on the grounds of the old Fort at what would become the corner of Jefferson and Linden in Old Town. In the county tax roles of 1867, Joe Mason had assets of $36,000 — more than all of the other residents of Larimer County combined!

Its not surprising then that in 1868, Mason and his partner Asaph Allen, a retired military officer, led a movement to have the Larimer County seat moved from Laporte to Fort Collins. But the fly in the buttermilk was that there wasn't any Fort Collins, fort or city. There was just Joe Mason's store and a handful of people who agreed with him.

However, Mason's voice was a powerful one. In addition to

being the largest business owner in Larimer County, Mason was also a county commissioner, and people listened to him. Mason went all over the valleys of the Cache La Poudre and the Big Thompson, selling his plan. "But Joe," the settlers would say, "There ain't no Fort Collins!" Mason would admit this was true, for now, but sooner than they thought, the lands of the army would be released to homesteading, and they would be able to build a proper city.

In September of 1868, the settlers were asked to vote on which city, or location, should be designated as the permanent location of the county seat. There were three candidates: Laporte, Old St. Louis, a settlement in the Big Thompson valley and the forerunner of the City of Loveland, and Fort Collins, the imaginary city located around the old fort. The records don't say who voted for what, but about 50 people did vote and they chose Fort Collins as the new county seat.

Within a month, all of the records were moved to the temporary county headquarters. It will come as no surprise that this was Joe Mason's store. They even moved the old jail that Benjamin Whedbee had built in Laporte to a corner of Joe Mason's lot.

As time rolled on, the hopes of the settlers that Congress would make quick work of the release of the military land, dwindled a little.

This bureaucracy prevented people from legally squatting on the land without the permission of the army. Mason was there by permission as were Auntie Stone, who had built a boarding house for the officers of Fort Collins in 1864; the gunsmith Henry Clay Petersen, and a few others. Everyone else was just dancing around the edges of the land, trying to figure out a way to get in.

The Mason and Allen General store was doing a brisk business with everyone in the valley. In the absence of a bank, the store served much the same purpose. Settlers were allowed to charge their supplies in advance of selling the harvest from their crops, usually to Mason and Allen themselves, who in turn would sell the surplus of the Poudre Valley's agriculture to an eagerly awaiting market in Denver and the mining camps to the west. Already the Poudre Valley was living up to part of its potential as a Colorado "Breadbasket," and with the addition of more acres to farming because of new irrigation ditches to flood the land, the prospects for a successful city called Fort Collins were even better.

The Outlaw Musgrove.

After the military reservation was closed and the soldiers pulled out, the people of the Poudre Valley were on their own. They had to depend on one another and always be ready for trouble. They weren't all noble souls with high ideals, these men of the West. Some of them were just plain stinkers!

The worst of the bunch was a gang of outlaws led by the man named Musgrove. His gang of thieves and cut-throats, as bad as any pirate in the Caribbean, terrorized northern Colorado and southern Wyoming from 1864 until 1868. They operated out of a hiding place at Bonner Spring, just west of Owl Canyon. The principal targets of the gang were horses and mules. Today that doesn't seem like such a huge crime, but in the 1860s, losing your horse or mule could be catastrophic. Remember that provisions and supplies for the early settlers

One of the original good guys, Abner Loomis, pioneered in Pleasant Valley west of Bingham Hill. He was a Fort Collins founder.

Fort Collins Library

had to be carried in wagons a distance of some 600 miles. If their team was stolen enroute, or driven off from the ranches, there was a good chance the settler would starve. The crime of horse stealing was at least as serious as murder, since it almost amounted to the same thing.

On the other hand, stealing horses and mules was tremendously profitable. A pair of mules brought from $350 to $700, with no questions asked, which made the risk to Musgrove worthwhile. Musgrove rustled horses all up and down the Cherokee Trail, mostly from the army and the Overland Stage. It was fashionable for thieves to pretend innocence and blame the thefts on the Indians. In the absence of hard evidence, they continued to get away with it.

But the gang never raided the settlers of the Poudre Valley. The reason they didn't was partly because the settlers were tough and dangerous people themselves, but mostly because of the warnings to stay out of the valley by one man — Abner Loomis.

Abner Loomis was one of the good guys He was a prominent founder of the city and was very well liked. Ansel Watrous wrote of him, "He was never quarrelsome, nor would he incite a row, but when a tough wanted to bully anybody, he invariably passed Ab Loomis by as a man too tough to quarrel with." A real John Wayne type.

By 1867 the outlaws had become such a nuisance that they sent out a Deputy U.S. Marshall from Denver to come to Larimer County, arrest Musgrove and break up his gang. In his search, the Deputy made a stop at Abner Loomis' ranch to ask a few questions. The Loomis ranch was in Pleasant Valley, just south of Bellvue at the bottom of Bingham Hill. Loomis told the Deputy that he could probably find Musgrove down in Laporte at one of the saloons. Thanking Abner for the tip, the Deputy rode off to do his duty.

The deputy reined in at the saloon that Loomis had mentioned. He checked his six-shooter, hitched up his belt, straightened his hat, and marched into the saloon.

The room was filled with at least a dozen, heavily armed, evil looking men. They were idly playing poker and billiards, but they stopped and looked at the deputy as he walked in. He had found Musgrove alright. What he hadn't counted on was finding him with his entire gang . . . all armed with pistols, rifles, shotguns and many assorted, long knives. The fact is, they were not overly frightened of the deputy.

Of course, the deputy did the only thing he could. He marched up to the bar, ordered a drink and then turned his back to the bar to face the leering faces. He smiled a pleasant grin, raised his glass and toasted the good health of the entire assembled multitude. Then he tossed down his drink and strode manfully out the door. Once outside he scrambled on to his horse and galloped away so fast he hardly heard the guffaws of laughter spilling out of the bar.

Musgrove was not amused. Who would have told the deputy where he was? "It must have been that snake, Abner Loomis!" growled Musgrove. "Maybe I'll just pay him a little visit."

The next morning, Musgrove rode over to the Loomis Ranch. He rode up to the cabin and pulled up next to the gate post where Loomis had hitched a fine mule that had cost him $250. Abner came out on the porch and invited Musgrove to come in for breakfast. Musgrove had a shotgun laid across the his saddle. When he raised up, as if to climb down, the shotgun went off and shot the mule.

Musgrove feigned surprise and shock. He told Abner that he was *so* sorry for shooting his mule. Then he turned and rode away at top speed. Loomis' first impulse was to shoot Musgrove, but he stopped to check his mule and when he looked up again, Musgrove had ridden out of site. But Abner Loomis was nothing if he was not patient. There would come another time.

During 1868, the Musgrove gang reached its most outrageous heights and the entire valley was anxious to get rid of them. There was also now a price on Musgrove's head. Horses, cattle, mules and anything else not nailed down was disappearing in great numbers. Something had to be done. So the US Marshall in Denver enlisted Abner Loomis in a plan to apprehend the outlaw. Loomis was happy to help since he still owed Musgrove for the dead mule.

In December, 1868, Loomis rode out to Owl Canyon. He was alone and unarmed when he rode into the outlaw camp. Musgrove came out, guns in hand. Loomis explained that he was on a peaceful mission and that he had news. So the outlaw let him stand down. Abner said that he had found a valuable horse and that he supposed the horse must belong to Musgrove. He invited Musgrove to ride back to Pleasant Valley with him to get it. The desperado figured that Loomis must be a fine fellow to ride all that way to do him a favor, and he saddled up and went back to Abner's ranch with him.

When the two men got back to the ranch, Abner suggested that they have a bite of lunch. So they went into the cabin and sat down to eat. On a prearranged signal, a deputy marshall named Haskell burst into the room, guns pulled, and arrested Musgrove. He placed the outlaw in irons and took him back to Denver to stand trial. Abner Loomis had his revenge.

Musgrove was much less fortunate. He arrived in Denver just when the city was on a campaign to get rid of all outlaws. When people learned that it was Musgrove himself in jail, a mob formed, grabbed Musgrove and took him out to the Larimer Street bridge and lynched him. And that was the end of the Poudre Valley's worst outlaw gang.

The Settlers Push On.

The settlers were still trying to make progress. Auntie Stone and Henry Petersen had been working to build a flour mill since 1866. They had even gone so far as to raise the money to build it. But when Petersen went back East to buy the equipment, he got mugged in Chicago and robbed of the $3,000 he was going to use for that purpose. He had to return to Fort Collins to raise more money, which he did, and in 1869, he and Auntie Stone finally got the mill opened.

The other principal event of 1869, was a tragic one. Joe Mason's partner in the store was Captain Asaph Allen. He had mustered out of the army in 1866 and had settled in the Poudre Valley. He was a very popular man and was regarded as someone who brought dignity and civilization to otherwise drab lives. In February, 1869 Allen got on the train at the rail-head in Cheyenne and went back East to buy goods for the store. Upon completion of his business he started back West. He got off the train in Baltimore and vanished into thin air. He was never seen again. It was believed that Allen was attacked and killed in a robbery for the money he carried. When news of the tragedy got back to Fort Collins, it threw the tiny settlement into a deep gloom of depression.

The pioneers would have to reflect with some irony that they had come West to get away from the snarling, swaggering East. They had been willing to endure hunger and cold; they had been prepared to meet the deadly threat of Indian attacks. Now, just as their hands grasped for the better lives for which they had fought, two of their own number, who had survived everything else out here on the wild frontier, had been victimized by the "civilized" world they left behind. But the settlers had come this far and had no intentions of quitting.

During this pensive time a valuable ally arrived on the scene. William C. Stover was one of Fort Collins' most important founders and a man who would help shape the destiny of the city for the next 30 years.

Stover. The Builder Of A City.

Bill Stover was born into one of the leading families of Virginia. When he was nine years old, the family moved to Indiana, where young Bill was educated. In the spring of 1860, Stover's father outfitted the young man with a team of good horses, wagon, clothing and provisions. He came West, and when he arrived in the Poudre Valley, he sold everything for a squatter's claim south of Loveland, just as he was celebrating his 19th birthday.

The following spring, 1861, Stover used all his money to buy seed for potatoes. He planted a crop in hopes of being able to sell it to the miners for a big profit. But he ran out of provisions before he could harvest his crop and had to dig up all his potatoes and eat them, leaving him with nothing to sell. When winter came his situation grew more desperate. He went to the cabin of a friend, who had also come from Indiana, and told him that he had no shoes. Indeed, his footwear was moccasins made out of old gunny

William C. Stover. One of the most important men in our history. He founded the Poudre Valley Bank, served as an officer of many city, county and state positions, and always tried to act in the best interests of Fort Collins.

Stover family archives

sacks. Worse, he didn't have any money to buy shoes. His friend said that he didn't have any money either, but he knew someone who did. The two of them walked all the way to

Boulder, and Stover borrowed eight dollars for a pair of boots. Then he made a pair of pants out of more gunny sacks and hunkered down for the winter, hoping he wouldn't starve.

In 1862 Stover got by doing odd jobs. In the fall he made a fair amount of money putting up hay. He paid back the eight dollars he had borrowed for his boots. The following year he sold his claim and took off for Virginia City, Montana, where a gold rush was in progress. Finally in 1864, Stover returned to South Bend, Indiana. But he was not going home to quit as many folks did. He was made of sterner stuff than that.

In the spring of 1865 Stover borrowed some money from his father. He combined it with what he had earned and bought a fleet of heavy freight wagons. He then loaded them up with provisions and merchandise and took off again for the gold fields in Montana. In Virginia City, flour was selling for 100 dollars a sack with everything else just as high. Stover made $5000 dollars on that trip. During the next two years, he made the 1800 mile round trip from Montana to St. Joseph, Missouri many times. This was not interstate highway travel. In fact, there were no roads at all, just hard times out here in the wilderness. But most often Bill Stover had a smile on his face.

Stover made lots of money selling supplies and provisions to the miners in Virginia City, Montana during the gold rush. In 1868 he returned to the Big Thompson, sold his freighting outfit, and paid back all the money he had borrowed from his father. In 1870 he moved to Fort Collins and, in the company of John Mathews, bought out Joe Mason and his store. Since this was the only general store in the area, he did a large and profitable business. In just 10 years Bill Stover had gone from nearly starving during the winter, to become one of the most prosperous settlers in the Poudre Valley. As the story of Fort Collins unfolded, it would be William Stover who would, most frequently, be its author.

An Upstart Colony On The Platte.

Just because the "City" of Fort Collins was tangled in a web of red tape in 1869, it didn't mean that the rest of the area was quiet. Thirty miles downstream of the Poudre River, near the confluence of the South Platte River, a new enterprise was taking shape. The Union Colony was established by Nathan Meeker under the supporting umbrella of his employer and friend, Horace Greeley. With the completion of a railhead near the colony, hundreds of people came west, and the colony grew rapidly. The settlers of the Poudre Valley could only watch with envy.

The Union Colony became the city of Greeley and was largely an experiment in social reform. From the beginning, the people in the East who were attracted to the colony where those who believed in the rather strict social, moral and religious environment that the colony demanded of its citizens. On the other hand it was also a land deal.

The man who acted as the land agent for the Union Colony at Greeley was a fellow named General R.A. Cameron, as in today's Cameron Pass. Along with William Byers, publisher of the Rocky Mountain News, they organized the land into lots and then sold them to people in the East who wanted to immigrate. By the end of 1870, Horace Greeley, himself, visited the colony and reported that there were already 700 families living there. The main advantage they had was the railhead. Fort Collins had none. Fort Collins also had only about 50 families, struggling along, and they had no railroad, no town and no tax base. But they continuously reminded the territorial legislature that they *were* the county seat.

It wasn't the legislature's fault. The operative word here is Territorial. Colorado didn't become at state until 1876. So, in 1870, the Territory of Colorado didn't get a lot of attention from a Congress in Washington that had its hands full dealing with reconstruction following the Civil War. Truthfully, the government had not even a particle of interest in the little 6,100 acres of the Fort Collins Military Reservation way out there beyond the frontier of civilization. After three years of frustrating delays, Joseph Mason is supposed to have said that he was sorry he hadn't gotten further away from Washington than he did, when he came out here in the first place.

Up until now, the founders of Fort Collins had done everything they could think of to legitimatize the existence of a town and make the government move more quickly to release the land. They had placed the county seat at Fort Collins figuring that would be more than enough to show their sincerity. Since the government ponderously ignored this obvious move, the founders figured that they needed something else. So they hatched an even more fantastic scheme.

What We Need Is Higher Education!

Somebody remembered that the federal government had passed a law clear back in 1862, called the Land Grant College Act. Basically the law said that states or territories could establish agricultural colleges and that the government would hand over 90,000 acres of government land that the university could rent or develop and keep all the money they made from it. To Joe Mason, the 29-year-old Larimer County Commissioner, that sounded like a good way to further the cause of Fort Collins, the non-existent city.

Mason and the rest of the Poudre Valley founders had watched with sincere concern while Greeley surged to the east. They were afraid that the colony would gobble up the idea of a land grant college. They also wanted some of that growth themselves. So, near the end of 1870, Mason and company went to Denver and embarked of a campaign of intense lobbying to get the legislature to designate Fort Collins as the site for the university.

They got much the same response as they had when they moved the county seat. "But Joe," the legislators said, "There ain't no Fort Collins!"

Apparently, the founders of Fort Collins were able to overcome this most obvious of objections, and when the smoke cleared the territorial legislature picked Fort Collins as the site for the agricultural college that we know today as Colorado State University. So, in some ways, the university actually precedes the town.

The Streets Are Sooo Wide!

Finally, more than five years after the request, the Congress approved a bill to release the lands of Fort Collins from the Army to the Department of the Interior. It was July of 1872. The moment the settlers had waited for all these years had come at last! Now town leaders really switched into high gear. Joe Mason, Henry Petersen, John Mathews and Bill Stover, joined forces with General Cameron, using his experience in

Franklin Avery's original 1873 plat of the new city of Fort Collins with streets that were 100 feet wide. Fort Collins Library

Part III: "Old Town" 1867-1878

89

the Union Colony, and formed the agricultural colony that became the city of Fort Collins. To these men were also added a number of people from Greeley. The most important of these were Jacob Welch and Franklin Avery. On December 9, 1872 a circular was published inviting anyone who was interested, a chance to buy residential and business lots in the town of Fort Collins.

An agricultural colony was a pretty common way of establishing towns on the frontier. Today we just do it on such a grand scale. The modern day equivalent would be the subdivision, in which a chunk of land is divided into lots and sold to the public. The chunk of land in this case was 3,000 acres of the old military reservation. The circular said that anyone of good moral character could buy a lot, or more than one lot if they wished to open a business, for $50 to $250 per lot. The circular said that the lots were appraised at twice their purchase price.

The intersection of Whedbee and Laurel. This picture was taken in 1927, 53 years after Avery laid out the original city. For all that time, it was unpaved and often impassable. The people loved Franklin Avery, but they hated those wide streets. Fort Collins Library

When the circular was published offering the lots for sale, one of our most important founders had already been hard at work. This was Franklin Avery. He was a surveyor by trade. It was Avery's job to lay out the new town and make a map or plat of it, so that people could see what they had purchased.

Avery started with an earlier plat of the area in which someone had laid out the streets that are in Old Town today. These streets were oriented to the river, which is why they run off in such funny directions. Avery used that plat as an original and proceeded to add his design to the remainder of the colony lands of 3,000 acres. However,

Visions Along The Poudre Valley

the streets he added were oriented north and south, east and west, on true compass lines. Old Town stayed cock-eyed, as it is even today. The plat goes south from the river all the way to Prospect Street, and east from Whitcomb all the way over to nearly Lemay. In keeping with the plans of the colony trustees, the downtown area was divided into business lots with residential lots surrounding it. As you got further from the center of town, the lots got bigger and ended up being 10, 20 and 40 acres parcels, suitable for farming and other agricultural interests.

Just about every newcomer to Fort Collins always remarks about the great wide streets we have in the older parts of town and wonder how they came to be. Well, Franklin Avery is the man who is responsible. In comparison to other towns, just about anywhere, these wide streets were unheard of. Avery did not have a crystal ball to predict that we would need those wide streets a hundred years later to accommodate the automobile, his idea was much simpler. His purpose in making the streets so wide was so that you could turn a team of horses hitched to a wagon around in the street without having to back up. Avery would say later that he had all this room to spare, and there was no reason not to use it. All of the streets are 100 feet wide, except for the major thoroughfares like College and Mountain. These are 140 feet wide.

How do you suppose the far-thinking, modern, enlightened new residents of Fort Collins liked their wide streets? They hated them . . . a lot! Complained about them all the time, because, none of these streets were paved, and most of the year they were a muddy, rutted mess. You couldn't cross the street without getting filthy!! It would be another 30 years before street paving appeared and for all of that time, at least as far as the streets were concerned, the people of Fort Collins thought Franklin Avery was an idiot.

Avery did more than just lay out the streets. He planned space for schools, parks, public buildings and for the campus of the university, right where they are today. He also gave the streets their names. He was a practical man, so he didn't spend a lot of time trying to be original. The streets that ran east and west, he named after trees . . . Oak, Olive, Magnolia, Mulberry, Myrtle, Laurel and so forth. The streets running north and south he named after the fellows who had been instrumental in the creation of the city . . . Mason, Petersen, Mathews, Loomis, Whitcomb, Whedbee, Stover and so forth. He finished his plat in January of 1873. Today the original can be seen on display at the Fort Collins Museum.

The colony that was the forerunner of Fort Collins was organized along some of the same lines as the Union Colony. In the circular announcing the formation of the new town, they wrote: "We have, at present, a post office, grist mill, two stores, a drug store, two blacksmith shops, a harness shop and two small hotels. What we need is: a newspaper, saw mill, hardware store, a bank, a livery stable and any number of good, industrious people."

They were just as specific about what they didn't want. "We do not need whiskey saloons or gambling halls. There is not a place in the county where liquor is legally or publicly sold, and we do not intend that it ever will be sold if we can help it. We wish to attract the most honest, religiously devout, law-abiding, hard-working, educated people that we can."

The immediate effect of the move to establish a colony was the sudden infusion of several hundred new people to the new town. Many buildings were erected, and business took a turn for the better. The very first elements of a society began to emerge. The divisions of the choice lots for both homes and businesses was typical of the American sense of fair play. This was going to be done in a fair and square way so that every-one had an equal chance to get a good site for his business or home.

First they took all of the lots that would be sold in the colony and threw them in a hat and drew out a fifth of them. Then they put all the names of the people who had put their money down into another hat and drew them out until all the lots were gone. Over the next few weeks they repeated the process several times until the entire 3,000 acres had been allo-cated. Thereafter a building boom ensued. In fact there was a sort of contest to see who could get his building up first. You will be interested to learn that the first of these new buildings to be completed was a lawyer's office.

Perhaps of greater importance was that all of this was responsible for setting off a feud between the Old Town and the New Town that would go on for the next 20 years. All of the people who had homesteaded the Poudre Valley in the old days had a tendency to sort of resent all of these newcomers from far away who brashly moved in and immediately started ordering them around and telling them what they could and could not do. About like today, not much has changed in that regard . . . only the issues.

The new town of Fort Collins grew so fast that in February of 1873, the Larimer County Commissioners granted a petition for a town council to be formed. With that Fort Collins officially achieved the status of a town. The commissioners appointed the first town trustees, which is the same thing as a city council. The first president of the trustees, meaning the first mayor of Fort Collins was the well-known and widely respected Benjamin Whedbee . . . Uncle Ben.

The new trustees of the town went to work right away. The first thing they did was to authorize the building of a road from the north end of College Avenue to the river, provided that the county agree to build a bridge over the river where the old power plant is today. The county built the bridge, and the road was completed. The second thing they did was to declare the cemetery dating from the time of the fort, to be a public nuisance. They ordered all the bodies to be exhumed and moved to the new Grandview cemetery at the west end of Mountain Ave. The old cemetery was right downtown and stood on the land that was eventually used for the old post office at the corner of College and Oak.

Bumpy Beginnings.

After waiting for over five years to finally establish the town of Fort Collins, the settlers were not willing to wait a second longer. But as it turned out it might have been better if they had. After a hopeful start and the influx of hundreds of new people in early 1873, national events and nature herself would conspire to rock the infant community to its very roots. In fact, it would have been easy . . . even probable, for the little town to have failed right then and there.

The first thing that happened was that the only bank in Fort Collins failed in the spring of 1873. In his history of Larimer County, Ansel Watrous wrote that this was because of the financial panic sweeping the country during this time. But the panic of 1873 did not occur until the fall and so it is likely that Watrous, always an eternal Pollyanna and very unwilling to say anything bad about the city of Fort Collins, was being overly kind. What probably happened was that this banker just stole all the money and then disappeared forever. At any rate, most of the cash in the whole county went with the banker and wiped out the savings of the farmers who were using that money to get them through until the harvest. This was much more serious than you might imagine. The real wealth of the Poudre Valley has always been in its land. From the beginning it was agriculture that drew people to the valley. The gold and silver mines were in the mountains. But all of those miners had to eat and they couldn't very well bring the food all the way from the East. It had to be grown locally. That's what the Poudre Valley did, serve as the breadbasket for the Front Range. When Fort Collins, was founded as a city in 1873, the heart of the economy was its agricultural industry. It was counted on to fuel the growth of the infant city. With all the cash reserves gone, the farmers were going to have to depend even more on a successful harvest.

The Skies Grow Dark!

1873 was just a beautiful year. The weather was just right for the crops. There was the right amount of rain at the right time, and the growing season was warm. The crops flourished. Principally it was wheat, hay and vegetables that covered the land and grew from the newly irrigated fields. As the summer rolled on, the farmers were glad to put the failure of the bank behind them and look forward to the best harvest they had ever had.

As the time for the harvest grew closer, the fields were a rich bounty of luxurious growth. The wheat fields spread out for miles with the heavy grain waving abundantly in the gentle breezes. Then, only days before the harvest, the skies blackened. The settlers watched the gathering storm with worried eyes for fear that heavy rains or even hail might damage their crops. But as the storm grew closer, the men and women saw with growing terror that these were not rain clouds at all. For sweeping up from the south and blotting out the sun were the bodies of billions and billions of grasshoppers.

No one had ever seen anything like it before in their lives.

Visions Along The Poudre Valley

The cloud of flying insects spread across the entire horizon and was miles deep. They fell upon the ripened grain, hay and vegetables and began to devour everything. The farmers tried everything . . . smudge pots, they even set fire to portions of their fields in hope that the smoke would turn the insects away. At the end, entire families were in the fields trying to stop the grasshoppers with their bare hands. They killed them by the millions, but uncounted millions more continued to eat everything in their path. No farm or ranch was spared. Before the plague had run its course, more than 30,000 square miles of the Colorado Front Range had been eaten right down to the bare ground. The land was laid to waste. This was much more serious than just losing their cash in a bank failure. Now the entire food supply of Colorado had been wiped out and the whole population of the territory faced starvation. There was very little money to buy food supplies and have it shipped by train from the East. Progress in the little town came to an abrupt halt. Many people gave up and left the area. Those that remained faced a bleak future.

To make matters worse, now the entire United States was gripped by the Panic of 1873, the worst depression in the history of the country, to that time. The New York Stock Exchange shut down for ten days. Thousands of banks failed. Tens of thousands of businesses went under and hundreds of thousands of people were suddenly unemployed. In Fort Collins, things could hardly have been worse. Everybody was broke. All of the crops had been eaten by the grasshoppers, and everybody was hungry. The little town was locked in a legal battle with Greeley over the water in the Poudre River. The ditch that supplied the town with their drinking water supply was leaking, and half the downtown area was under water. What's more, the citizens of Fort Collins had voted to prohibit liquor sales the previous May, and everybody was in a sullen, ugly mood.

Mason Moves On.

Clearly Joseph Mason was an honest man. One of his partners in business, as well as good personal friend, was F.W. Sherwood, an early settler and successful rancher. Over a period of several years, the two men did business together, buying and selling horses and cattle. Mason did most of the buying, and Sherwood kept the books. When they finally dissolved the partnership, Sherwood told Mason that he had to pay $6,250.50 for his share of the profits. Mason promptly wrote out a check for exactly $6,250 and NO cents, saying in the process that he was happy to pay what he owed but would never pay the fifty cents because Sherwood must have made a mistake. It was a huge joke between the two of them, that was shared by most of the town for years. But the question of real honesty was never a question at all.

In 1868, when the county voted to move the seat to Fort Collins, the county commissioners, including Joe Mason, had all the records, papers, safe, even the jail, moved to the site of the old fort. Where do you suppose the county set up shop? Right again. It all went to the building called Old Grout, the humble store of good old Joe Mason. For several years, the effective county seat headquarters was this building, that stood at the corner of Jefferson and Linden street in Old town.

Then, after all of this, and partly because of the death of his partner, Asaph Allen, Mason sold the store to William C. Stover and John Mathews in 1870. He had gone to all the trouble to get the county seat moved to Fort Collins to protect his interests in his store, and then just sold it. A curious turn of events, but Joseph Mason had other ideas.

Besides being a sooper dooper prime mover in the affairs of Larimer County, Joseph Mason also had a personal life. In 1868, he met Luella Blake, the daughter of a settler family who lived in the area. In 1870, they were married. Mason was 30 years old and his wife was just 20. Together they had four children. The oldest daughter died at the age of 22. Two younger boys died at the age of two and twelve of smallpox. Only Joseph Junior survived. The family of that Mason son continues to survive in Fort Collins today.

Presumably, Joe Mason enjoyed a great deal of his personal time during this period because he didn't reappear in a public capacity until 1871. In that year, he was again drawn away from his farm located, along north College Avenue, to once again attend to the business of Larimer County.

In 1871, Joe Mason was elected as sheriff of Larimer County. He was re-elected again in 1873. During this time,

Joseph Mason was the Matt Dillon of the Poudre Valley. He was a very busy man. For the most part, there were no more real problems with the Indians, but now people were beginning to move into the area in larger numbers. With the establishment of Fort Collins as a real town in 1873, growth came in larger doses. There was a lot of construction on irrigation projects, and so there were gangs of workers in camps all around Fort Collins. There were also ranch hands who worked on the neighboring spreads. This meant a lot of rough young men got "fixed up" to come to town on a Saturday night. It was Joseph Mason's job to keep a lid on all this, and there is every reason to believe that he did the job very well.

In 1873, Mason was appointed as postmaster for the area by the President of the United States. Never being a person to keep his irons out of the fire, he also continued to be engaged in commerce. In those days, valuable people like Mason were permitted to do all sorts of things that they couldn't do today. That same year, 1873, he bought into the flour mill in Fort Collins, that had been started by Auntie Stone and Henry Clay Petersen in 1866.

Happy Jack.

In the midst of all the problems that the infant community of Fort Collins was suffering through, it was not immune to the seedier side of life on the frontier. Along with the settlers, the solid citizens who had come to the Poudre Valley to stay and make homes, there also came into the valley the crooks, the thieves and the outlaws to prey on people. Such a man wandered into Fort Collins in the summer of 1873. He was known only as Happy Jack. Don't let his name fool you, he was a truly bad man, and his story has become a permanent part of our folklore.

Happy Jack worked around the valley at odd jobs, never staying with anything for very long. However horses and livestock started to disappear from the nearby farms and ranches. The general feeling was that Happy Jack was to blame. The sentiment got so strong that a warrant for his arrest was issued, and it became the job of the Sheriff of Larimer County, Joseph Mason, to go out and pick him up. Mason brought

Happy Jack into Fort Collins, but the county judge ruled that there was not enough evidence to try him, so Mason had to let him go, even though he was convinced they had the right man. He did the only thing he could. In classic Western language he told Happy Jack that Fort Collins was not big enough for both of them and that he had until sundown to clear out.

Happy Jack left Fort Collins and headed west into the Poudre Canyon. Along the way he passed the cabin of a family named Day. Mr. Day was not home at the time. Mrs. Day extended hospitality to the stranger and fed him a meal. Happy Jack thanked her by criminally assaulting her and then beating her senseless. He left the cabin with a sneer on his face. When Mr. Day returned home and discovered what had happened to his wife, he sent word back to Fort Collins. Sheriff Mason was out the door with a deputy in two minutes flat and was wearing out horses to pick up the trail of Happy Jack.

On the night of the second day of the search, Joe Mason came upon Happy Jack, sound asleep under a tree along the trail. The official records only say that Mason took Happy Jack into custody. The chances are that this business of "taking into custody" did not include reading Happy Jack his rights. The most amazing thing of all was that Joseph did not kill the man on sight. Nevertheless, within minutes Happy Jack was handcuffed, leg-ironed and thrown, beaten and bloody, onto the back of his horse.

Along the way, they passed the very homestead of the Day family. Mason reined in the horses and called Mrs. Day from the cabin. When she came out Mason asked her if this was the mad who had assaulted her. She said that it most certainly was. With that Mason hauled Happy Jack off his horse, drug him over to the corral, and tied him to a post. The Western pioneers took a very dim view of having their women abused, so Mason took out his rifle, handed it to Mrs. Day and told her to shoot him. Happy Jack cringed in terror as Mrs. Day took the rifle, cocked it, and pointed it right between his eyes. There was a long moment as Mrs. Day stood there with Western Justice in her hands and a grim purpose in her heart. Happy Jack screamed in agony for Mrs. Day to spare him. She wanted to shoot him. She really did, and Mason seemed perfectly willing to stand by quietly and let her do it. According to the records, Happy Jack threw up and wet his pants. With that Mrs. Day slowly lowered the rifle.

Sheriff Mason brought Happy Jack back to Fort Collins where word of the incident had spread through the valley. Sentiment was running high to hang Happy Jack. Mason locked him up in a room on the second floor of the Old Grout building that stood on the corner of Jefferson and Linden. During the night a dozen men gathered outside. Then they went in and dragged Happy Jack out. They threw a rope over one of the roof beams and around Jack's neck. They were determined to wring a confession out of him for stealing horses. Assaulting women was not a hanging offense, but stealing horses was, and the mob was in an angry mood. Several times during the night the crowd hauled Happy Jack out, swearing that this time they were going to hang him. But Happy Jack never confessed to anything.

The following night Jack complained that his leg irons were too tight and a sympathetic deputy loosened them a little, just enough for Jack to be able to slip the chains off his boots and make good an escape in the cover of darkness. When his escape was discovered, a posse took off in hot pursuit. The accounts of the chase vary. Most people came to believe that Jack really did escape and never returned. But one story that has been whispered down through the years is that the posse caught up to Happy Jack at the natural stone fort you see on I-25 between here and Cheyenne. The story says they hung him and concealed his body in an unmarked grave. None of the men who were part of the posse would ever say what happened.

Throughout this part of the history of the Poudre Valley, we have talked about progress and true civilization coming to the new town of Fort Collins. Now, in the midst of it, here is a story that sounds like any Hollywood western. What we learn from this is that the settlers who were intent upon having a home here on the mile high bench lands at the foot of the great mountains were strong-willed, strong-minded people. They were willing to endure and to deal with the worst that man and nature could throw at them, but only until they could produce, from the strength of their own characters, a better life for themselves and their families.

The Colorado and Southern railroad, in cooperation with the great Union Pacific, connected Fort Collins to the rest of the world in 1877. Even though this picture was not taken in 1877, it's still an accurate reproduction of work crews laying the track and extending the line.   Paramount Pictures

The Tide Turns And The Whistle Blows.

Clearly, 1873 was a momentous year for the new town of Fort Collins. Not only was it almost sunk by financial crisis and grasshopper plagues, but also by the men who had come West to build nothing, only to prey on the tiny community. With the abandonment by so many of the town, those that remained became close knit and determined. Now the tide began to turn in the settler's favor.

Progress after the disastrous year of 1873 was not entirely retarded. Those with stouter hearts and bigger bankrolls from the East still found their way into Fort Collins. In the spring of 1874 a new bank was founded by A.K. Yount. The farmers planted again and hoped for better results this year. They were determined to protect themselves from the scourge of grasshoppers that were sure to show up again before the harvest.

Using some very rudimentary pesticides that would probably make any modern environmentalists pass out in a dead faint, the farmers armed themselves against the grasshoppers.

They set up a series of smudge pots, built little dams they could open and flood the fields, anything to kill the diminutive pests. When the insects did arrive at the end of the summer, the settlers used everything in their tiny arsenals and were able to harvest, not all, but a fair share of their crops. When the grasshoppers came again for a third year in 1875, the stout agricultural community wiped them out and brought in most of their crops. The pioneers took a great deal of pleasure in doing this, and no crop has ever been lost to grasshoppers since that time. But it was often one step forward and two back. 1875 was the year that gold was discovered in the Black Hills of South Dakota, and people left in droves to seek their fortune. Something was missing that the town needed in order to call themselves a successful city.

Since the town of Fort Collins was established in 1873, the citizens of Larimer County had been wistfully looking forward to the day when a railroad would be built from Denver to connect with the big Union Pacific tracks in Cheyenne. The railroad was the most modern means of transportation on earth. It was the umbilical that would connect Fort Collins with the outside world and would offer farmers and ranchers a way to ship their surplus goods, crops and livestock to a waiting market. A railroad meant prosperity and permanence for a western community. Without it, the town had very little chance to grow and flourish. The railroad was the key since their were no real roads, cars, trucks or other transportation services that we take for granted today.

The spring of 1877 opened hopefully. The word came that all the preliminaries had been completed and that a new railroad company had been founded by a Coloradoan named W.A. Loveland. That name has sort of a familiar ring to it, doesn't it? Anyway, Loveland formed the Colorado Central in partnership with the great Union Pacific. While Loveland's Chief Engineer, Captain Berthoud, was grading and surveying the route north from Longmont, the Union Pacific pushed south from Cheyenne.

All through the summer of 1877, the work crews labored to lay track. By the end of September, the smoke from the construction trains could be seen on the bluffs north of Fort Collins. There were only a few hundred people in town, but they were beside themselves with anticipation. They couldn't wait. The little town of Old Saint Louis, south and west of Fort Collins, was so excited that they moved their whole town to be in the way of the railroad. They gave it a new name . . . Loveland.

The city of Fort Collins prepared for the arrival of the railroad by granting it a right of way through town on Mason Street, right where it is today. They also donated land for a depot and for switching yards. The depot was built right off College Avenue at Laporte and Mason. The switching yards are still being used, much to the irritation of modern commuters. There is hardly a person today who has not been delayed from getting to some very important appointment by the passage of a big lumbering train, right down Mason Street and through the middle of town. Nowadays we tend to regard these delays as a terrible inconvenience and wonder who the idiot was to put a train track right in the middle of all this traffic. The answer, of course, is that we did it to ourselves. The right of way and the land were all freely, gladly and unanimously given by the determined early residents of Fort Collins, to accommodate the almighty Iron Horse and bring the town into contact with the outside world.

On October 8, 1877 the first construction train rolled into town. Everybody turned out to see the train arrive. It was an occasion of grand celebration. It was as if the people had just won the Superbowl and the World Series all rolled into one. They were all wild with delight and they partied all day and into the night. A few days later the first trainload of goods arrived in town. It was a boxcar full of merchandise for Bill Stover's store.

This was the day on which Fort Collins ceased to be an unknown settlement in the wilderness and became a frontier community. For all of the immigrants who wanted to come West, they now had a "highway" on which to travel. All of the home residents now had a way to ship their surplus products to wider and better markets.

More than ten years had passed since the closing of the old military fort. Over half of that time had been spent in getting the 6,000 acres of the military reservation released for homesteading. The pioneers of Fort Collins had endured much, but the settlers had lived through it all, on their own, and with no government programs, disaster relief or any of the other safety nets that we would demand in these modern times. They made their own social security, passed laws that seemed good to them and worked together to build a better future.

Now with the arrival of the railroad there was reason for real optimism. That belief was well founded because every day the train rolled into town bringing new families who came with everything they had, prepared to roll up their sleeves and get to work.

"Boom Town"
1878-1899

T HE RAILROADS . . . brought reality to the concept
of a nation that could span a continent, and grasp
its "Manifest Destiny". In 1864, it took 12 weeks to
make the back-breaking, harrowing and dangerous trip
by wagon train from the Mississippi River to the Poudre
Valley. By 1869, you could go from the nation's Capital
to the Golden Gate in relative comfort in days, and with
the enormous advantage of bringing with you everything
of value you owned. It was as if some gigantic inner
voice had spoken to the entire nation and said "OK,
everybody get up and slide to the West a thousand
miles!" The fact is, the very best families of the East,
went to the very best places of the West. Among these
was the vastly undervalued Poudre Valley.

A thing of beauty. The railroad comes to Fort Collins. With its arrival, the Poudre Valley boomed.

Fort Collins Library

"Get On The Road, A-Rolling West, Out To The Great Unknown"

In the years that followed the end of the Civil War in 1865, a United States of America began to expand in all directions. The 35 million people of the country had the feeling that a lot had been settled with the war and that they could now get on with the business of living freely in a free country.

Nowhere did the promise of opportunity burn brighter than in the American West. The government promised free land to anyone who could claim it and improve it, and literally millions of people from America and around the world took the offer and the plunge into the unknown wilderness.

The people came west for all sorts of reasons . . . for gold, for land, for religious and political freedom. But everyone of them believed in their hearts that they would be able to build, from their own hands, a better life for themselves and their children.

As the hordes of people moved west, American enterprise came with them, establishing a network of railroads that gave easy, fast, reasonably inexpensive transportation. People who

Part IV: "Boom Town" 1878-1899

wanted to come west, now had a highway to take them there, and they flowed toward the setting sun in their endless numbers.

In October of 1877, the highway came to the little town of Fort Collins with the arrival of the Colorado Central railroad. By the time that the railroad finally did chug into town on Mason Street, the population of the town was down to about 800 people.

The arrival of the railroad gave Fort Collins an immediate shot in the arm. Everyday, men with their families and all possessions, including their livestock, arrived at the old train station at the corner of Mason and Laporte. They were prepared to stay and make the best of it, but very few of them had a particle of an idea how hard this was going to be. Let me try and give you a better picture of what it must have been like.

Imagine that you are a family from the East, say Pennsylvania. You are prosperous and used to living on a well-ordered farm with wooden fences. You have plenty of rain to make the crops grow, friends and family all about you, a fully functional court system, laws, organization, daily newspapers and a social infrastructure. Now you learn that the whole western half of the country is just ripe for the taking, unlimited opportunities, not very many people, the ground floor to making a fabulous fortune. So you sell your farm, gather everything you think you might need, assemble the family, put all your money in your deepest pocket, and pile everything onto a train headed west. A few days later, you are unceremoniously dumped at a dinky little train station in the middle of nowhere. You look around you and see perhaps a hundred wooden buildings and houses that comprise the entire community of this place to which you have come, called Fort Collins, Colorado. The streets are vast expanses of grimy dust. It's too hot . . . too dry . . . to damn primitive. There are hardly any trees at all. You don't know anybody. Your family looks at you as if you are the stupidest man that ever walked the face of the earth, and your wife wants to know what you have gotten them into. Welcome to the Poudre Valley in the year 1878.

The Rush To The Poudre Valley Is On!

Once they were here there was nothing for the new settlers to do but roll up their sleeves and get to work. Everyone went to work taking part in the huge task of building a proper city. The expansion turned a little, tiny village into a Boom Town, almost overnight, but it was not easy. As a matter of fact, the early growth of Fort Collins was the most chaotic, disorganized, unrestrained, unplanned and unrehearsed mess you ever saw. It was like a huge symphony orchestra of brilliant musicians, all playing their own song and trying to convince all of their fellow musicians, in between breaths, to play along with them. People were building homes, churches and farms. They were trying every conceivable form of business venture and literally wallowing in the cultural diversity that was available to them.

Many of the people who arrived were not even Americans. They came from everywhere. The British had been a part of the West for many years with their investments in land, offering places to send their wild young people for a little seasoning and a freshman course in the school of hard knocks. They were joined by the Germans, Scandinavians, French, Russians and Italians. All were welcomed. The town had almost nothing. It needed just about everything. When newcomers arrived, if they had money in their pockets, were honest, hardworking and willing to become a part of the community, they were accepted as equals, or almost equals by everyone. Most of the world did not practice anything like that kind of tolerance, but in the American West it was pretty common, and especially so in Fort Collins. It is one of the bedrock traditions that still is a part of our character today.

In 1878, the signs of a modern, progressive city began to emerge. One of the first of these was the appearance of a newspaper. It was called the Courier, later it was called the Express Courier, and in 1945 it became the Coloradoan. The Courier was established in June, 1878 by a man named Ansel Watrous. Most of you probably think that Ansel Watrous is just a campground in the Poudre Canyon, but he was a very real and important man.

Ansel Watrous became the voice of Fort Collins for the next 30 years. He was a quiet and unassuming man. He wrote his newspaper in a concise and literary manner. In 1910, partly because he was frustrated when no one else took up the job, he sat down and wrote his 500 page History of Larimer County. Watrous was afraid that so much of our early history would be

Ansel Watrous was the editor of Fort Collins' leading newspaper for 30 years. He wrote the first history of Larimer County in 1910. Fort Collins Library

lost if he didn't, and he was right.

By 1879, the boom was in full swing. Outside the city limits, meaning beyond Whedbee or Laurel streets, there was a thriving, highly experimental and exciting agricultural revolution in progress. The big irrigation companies were digging ditches and bringing water to thousands of acres of prime land to the south. The farmers had adjusted to the scarcity of natural water, and were planting the first of the apples, plums, cherries, strawberries and other fruits. They were raising cattle and growing wheat and hay. In the valley of the Horsetooth, where the reservoir is today, a bustling quarry had opened to bring high quality, native red and brown sandstone to the hands of the eager builders in town.

Of course, no where was the growth and expansion more evident then in the town of Fort Collins itself. In the 12 months of 1879, about a hundred buildings and homes, most of them built of stone, were completed. The most important of these included the first building on the campus of Colorado Agricultural and Mechanical College. It was called Old Main, and it stood near the corner of College and Laurel Streets. The first class of students, all 25 of them, started school in the fall. There were other landmark buildings as well. Among them was the Tedmon House Hotel. It was built at the corner of Linden and Jefferson. It had 65 rooms on three stories, and they advertised that they had a bathroom for every floor. For the next 30 years, the Tedmon would be the premier hotel in northern Colorado. It was finally torn down to make room for the new Union Pacific railroad line, and today is just a grassy

Visions Along The Poudre Valley

park on that corner. Another of the most remembered constructions of 1879, was the home of Franklin Avery on Mountain Avenue. It was also built of native stone and today is preserved intact by the historical society. The Avery House is available for tours most days of the week.

The Wild West.

Larimer County was filling up fast. In 1870, the population of the county was 878. Five years after the railroad arrived, the population had mushroomed to over 8,000 people. The population of Fort Collins had gone from a few hundred in 1870 to 1,356 in 1880. By 1883, it would grow to over 2,000 people. The majority of all this growth came in the years between 1878 and 1883 caused by the arrival of the railroad in Fort Collins. The citizens of the county were very proud of their solid-looking, progressive county seat.

Thousands of young men had poured into the county to work on the ditch gangs, railroad crews, and quarries. Now where do suppose all those people went when the wanted to

Looking southwest along Linden Street from Jefferson Street. This was nearly all of Fort Collins in 1881. The large building in the background is the opera building. The steeple of a church can be seen, and Old Grout is in the foreground.

have a good time? Right! Fort Collins was the big time, especially for all those red-blooded, able-bodied young men who came into town looking for relaxation, entertainment, liquor and girls . . . not necessarily in that order. Fort Collins was doing a land office business with all these men and people were getting rich from the money they spent!

So, for the six breathtaking years between 1878 and 1883, the words Fort Collins and The Wild West meant the same thing. It was just like you see in the movies. Fort Collins was a wild, wide open town . . . a western frontier Sodom and Gomorra. Everybody from all over the county came to town on a Saturday night to whoop it up . . . also on Monday, Tuesday, Wednesday and so forth. At any given time there were at least 12 houses of ill-repute in full operation. These "Dirty Dozen" were accompanied by saloons, gambling halls, arcades, restaurants, and hotels. There were plenty of people to fill up every building to bursting. All through the day and night you could see men galloping their horses down the street while singing at the top of their lungs.

Mostly it was a tremendous amount of fun! The vast majority of these people had come from the East where life was pretty dull and stuffy. But *this,* this was heaven! For once, all the people who wanted to throw caution to the wind and all the rules of society right out the window, along with their clothes, outnumbered the people who wanted to stop them. Think of it as a sort of modern day amusement park, with guns.

Between the years of 1878 and 1883, Fort Collins had the reputation of being the most obliging town in these parts. It was certainly all of that. The most amazing thing was that it lasted so long. The party went on for six years before the city of Fort Collins and its solid citizens got it shut down. Actually they didn't really get it all stopped even then. Liquor was not outlawed for good until 1896, and the prostitutes were not all run out of town until 1899. But for now, the boom was just beginning, and people were enjoying a period of prosperity of the kind that they had come out to the West for in the first place.

Let me help you imagine what must have been going through people's minds in those days. We eavesdrop on a conversation that could have happened on the streets of Fort Collins between some of our founders. Think of yourself standing at the corner of College and Mountain in the winter of

1880, February 3. It was a cold night and the streets were dark because there were no street lights. But there were many lights on in most of the buildings in the center of town and the sound of music from many pianos and other instruments spilled out into the night. The streets were not deserted. Men and women strolled along the wooden sidewalks, and many horses and wagons were hitched to posts.

Inside a small restaurant, tucked away in a corner, two men sat at a table sipping coffee. Both were a part of Fort Collins from the beginning. One of them was Joseph Mason, the acknowledged "first" citizen of the town.

The other was Bill Stover. Since buying out Mason's interest in the general store, Stover had gone on to found the Poudre Valley Bank. He was, at this time, president of the bank with wide business interests, and was the city's leading businessman. "Business good, Bill?" asked Joe Mason over the rim of his cup.

"Too good! We're working night and day! I'm thinking about building a bigger bank."

Mason slurped his coffee and then said, "I've been thinkin' that the railroad's got its bad points too."

"How so?" asked Stover. "We've never had it so good since the railroad came to town."

"Maybe," said Mason, "But it ain't turning out like I thought it would. We're attracting a lot of the wrong kind of people. We've got more whorehouses than we do hotels."

"I know, I know," said Stover with a wave of his hand. "We're gonna' have to do something about that."

"The trouble with you and a lot of others," said Mason, evenly, "Is that you're makin' so much money from all the men coming to town from the ranches and quarries and the like, that you don't want to give it up."

"Now, Joe," protested Stover, "You know I don't own any of those saloons."

"Maybe not, but you've got your finger into every business in town with that bank of yours."

"It's all legitimate business," said Stover.

"Well, the saloons are legitimate. The bordellos are legitimate. The trouble is . . . They ain't *right!* We ought to close 'em down."

"You sound like my wife," said Stover with a smile. "She's

going to all these temperance meetings and nags me all the time about the saloons and the liquor and the bordellos. And besides, in case you haven't noticed, the city needs all sorts of things like a sewer system and running water, and street improvements and a fire department. Those things take money to build and a lot of the taxes we get to build them come from the same businesses you want to outlaw."

Joe Mason thought for a minute and then said, "That may be true, but people didn't come out here to the West to raise their families in a cesspool full of sin and corruption. It has a bad effect on the children."

"Yeah, I know," agreed Stover, "but it's just as hard on the children and the families to have no running water and not enough schools and school teachers. It's gonna cost us and we need all the tax revenue we can get."

Just then a man burst into the restaurant and yelled to the diners, "Jacob Welch's building is on fire!"

Instantly, the restaurant emptied out as everyone ran to see what they could do to help. As Joseph Mason and Bill Stover hurried down the street, Stover said, "We've got to get a fire department!"

After the fire in 1881, Jacob Welch rebuilt his store at the corner of College and Mountain Avenues. This is the new store as it appeared in 1885.

Fort Collins Library

The Welch building stood at the corner of Mountain and College, where the Stone Lion Bookstore is today. It was a beautiful two story dry goods store, one of the biggest in town. Quickly it was engulfed in smoke and flames, and the efforts by all the volunteers who tried to help did little to get the fire knocked down. The building also served as the living quarters of the Welch family and others who lived on the second floor. Altogether there were ten people in the structure when the fire broke out, all of them were looking for a way out as thick smoke engulfed the rooms. And everyone did get out except for the two employees of the business. They were Andrew Hopkins and Tillie Irving, both clerks. They were a handsome couple and everyone had hopes that one day they would marry. But on this night, all of their hopes ended, and both of them were killed in the fire. Andrew was overcome with smoke as he went down the stairs, and Tillie never got out of her room.

Beyond the terrible cost in human lives, the burning of the Welch building was a severe loss to the city of Fort Collins. The building burned to the ground with all its contents and the loss was put at $50,000, a huge amount of money in 1880. The fire was the catalyst that caused the citizens of Fort Collins to move into action. The city council established a fire department. But the problem was that the fire department couldn't do much more than shout "Fire", because they had no water to fight fires.

The Passing Of Joseph Mason.

Just a year following the fire at the Welch building, on February 11, 1881, Joe Mason was visiting the ranch of his pal Fred Sherwood located at about where I-25 and Prospect Street are today. As he was changing the tack on one of his horses, it kicked him in the head. He went down like a rock. Sherwood carried him inside the house and a doctor was summoned. Mason never regained consciousness. He hung on for a few days, and then he died. He was 42 years old.

Joseph Mason dreamed the big dream, dared the great adventure. He was a pioneer at 15, rancher at 21, county commissioner at 22. When he was 28, he conducted his campaign to move the county seat to Fort Collins to protect his interests as the most prosperous man in the county.

At the age of 31, he was elected sheriff of the county. You have to wonder why a man who was so successful in business chose to take the job of sheriff, which paid practically nothing. Maybe it was because he wanted to make sure that nothing or nobody messed up the huge jump-start he had given northern Colorado, and the only way to do that was to become the arm of the law.

There is no telling what Joseph Mason would have accomplished if he had lived out his full life. But on the day he died in 1881, Fort Collins had become a real city. The railroad had come and new people, good people, were coming here to live in great numbers. They came with their families, their furniture, their stock and trade. They came with everything they had, and they came to stay. This new generation of builders would never know the man who had made it all possible.

He was our first lawman, first citizen, first family, and first to be a success in the wilderness. From bare land with nothing but prairie dogs, to a city that has grown to 100,000 people, all the lines of our town head straight back in history to one man . . . Joseph Mason. The one with the most perfect vision along the Poudre Valley.

The Appearance Of The City Infrastructure.

Not only were the citizens of Fort Collins demanding social and moral improvements, they were also demanding that the town be as progressive as any other city in the United States. They wanted the best of everything and were willing to pay for it in taxes and municipal bonds. Through all the ups and downs of the economy and the fortunes of people who were affected by it, the city of Fort Collins moved forward to provide itself the necessary civic improvements they wanted. It was an extensive list.

With all the excitement and enthusiasm of creating something brand new and beautiful — where nothing existed before, the people of Fort Collins; newly arrived and veteran pioneers, young and old, men and women, spit on their hands and went to work with the industry of an ant hill.

In 1880 the city of Fort Collins, aided and abetted by an informed and very vocal public, commenced on a capital improvement program that would take them all the way to the end of the century. Among the first things people wanted was entertainment. Not the kind of entertainment that was going on in Old Town every night, but of the type that was culturally rewarding, spiritually uplifting, family entertainment. Nothing would do except an opera house. Every western city had to have one. Good entertainment was hard to come by out on the edge of civilization and the people of the West went out of their way to make sure they got all they could. So they built opera houses, even if not a single opera was every performed in them. Fort Collins was no exception, and in 1880 the opera house opened on College Avenue in the same location as its modern day namesake, the Opera Galleria. That same building was used for performances and meetings right up until the late 1970s.

Next, the people considered the matter of fire protection. This included a sewer system and running water. Up until this time the people were sort of on their own to supply water for their needs. They got their water, for daily cooking and drinking, from the city's water wagon that went from street to street selling it for 25 cents a barrel. Well, that wasn't going to get it. Even given that the citizens were getting a little tired of the town burning down every few months, they were really getting tired of having to lug water from a wagon everyday. This was very tedious, and the people were certain that a town with a railroad and 2000 people, really ought to have a water system. After all, these were the 1880s!

The opera house was very popular for stage shows, concerts and public meetings. This picture from 1883. The opera house was actively used into the 1970s.
Fort Collins Library

Building a sewer system and providing running water to the town is a much bigger project than its sounds. You can build all the houses you want and lay them out neatly on city streets, but you really don't have anything very permanent until you put in a municipal water system. It's the foundation block of a city infrastructure. And the cost was astronomical for those days and for a town of just under 2000 people. A basic water system was going to cost $105,000. The city held a big election in 1882 and to everyone's mutual surprise, it passed.

The original water plant was built on Overland Trail, close to the river, the city's water supply. The building is still there today and preserved so you can see it. Altogether the city installed 43,000 feet of water lines, 20 fire hydrants, and 15 water gates. The whole system was completed and tested and then put into service on June 7th, 1883. The specifications

The water wagon went from street to street providing water for cooking and drinking for Fort Collins homes. A barrel full of water cost 25 cents.

called for the water pressure to be enough to send water to the top of a three story building. In fact, the geyser of water that spurted from a fire hydrant, downtown, shot 115 feet in the air. The system covered all of the today's downtown section and a few blocks in all directions. It meant that the fire department could now do more than just look at fires and direct traffic. It was also enough to give people the wonderful luxury of running water, inside the house. The filthy old water wagon was retired and never used again by the progressive city of Fort Collins.

Along with the water system came a new status for the town of Fort Collins. In 1883 the population went over 2,000 people. This meant that the city could apply to the state for an improved municipal status. This designation was called a "City of the Second Class." That sort of sounds like getting the silver medal, but it was a step up since it improved the city's ability to issue bonds and pay for civic improvements. The whole town was taking on a much more civilized air. The fire department moved into the new City Hall, that had been built in 1881. It's the same building that has been privately restored to its original condition and can be seen any day in Old Town on Walnut Street.

Many of the buildings that we still see and are still in use today were built during this period. The main reason why many of the buildings are still around is because they were built out of the native stone that was quarried just a few miles away. It's also the reason why Fort Collins, Colorado has about the largest collection of authentic western frontier architecture that still remains in the country.

But that still doesn't exactly tell us why these buildings were built. In many cases, they were built to keep up with the Jones', to compete in business with other companies. The concept of mass marketing, advertising and the media to carry the messages were still a half century away, so people competed by having beautiful buildings. Nowhere was this more evident than in the financial community.

Better Buildings Make Better Banks.

Bill Stover and Charles Sheldon had gotten together back in 1878 to found a bank. They went through a couple of buildings, neither of which survive today. But they were motivated to build a better building after Franklin Avery had opened his very nice bank building on College Avenue across from the Opera House. So in 1883, Stover met the competition of Avery's First National Bank by combining with another pio-

neer, Abner Loomis, to form the Poudre Valley Bank. They built the Loomis Andrews building at the corner of Linden and Walnut in Old Town. It turned out to be a classic. It was a three story structure that cost $32,000 to build. It had a huge vault, cherry wood railings and brass wickets at the teller's windows. Everyone thought that it was a beautiful build-

Built by William C. Stover in 1881, and costing $32,000, the Poudre Valley Bank was the leading Fort Collins financial institution. Years later it became the Linden Hotel. The entire building was restored in 1994 for a cost of $2 million. Fort Collins Library

ing. Just the place to put your money. Serious competition for Avery who began to plot his next move.

Of course, you may know this building yourself. It's the

very same Linden Hotel Building that has recently received a total renovation. The building now looks substantially the same as it did in 1883. It looks wonderful and the building is now proudly back at work. The money is not the same as 1883, however. The current restoration of the building cost more than two million dollars.

Now it was Avery's turn to keep up with the times. He bought the lot at the corner of Linden and Mountain and, after a number of false starts, he built his classic building. It was ultimately designed and built by Fort Collins leading architect, a man named Montezuma Fuller. He designed many homes and buildings in Fort Collins that still are in use today. He built Avery's building out of the native sandstone where he had a big stone lion carved into the rock and the word "Bank" chiseled into the lintel above the entrance. Although the building today is the home of several retail stores, the stone lion and the word "Bank" still adorn at the entrance to the Avery Building on the corner of Linden and Mountain at the mouth of Old Town Square.

There were many others who followed the lead of Stover and Avery and built beautiful buildings of their own. Nearly all of them are faithfully preserved today. When you see them in Old Town Square, on College Avenue and other places around town, it doesn't seem they are so old, but all of this was a part of Boom Town, over a hundred years ago.

The Old Fort's Last Building.

In modern times we have learned to be very careful of our heritage buildings and famous sites. However, in the 1880s, the greatest enemy of these structures were the people of Fort Collins themselves. The way thinking ran in those days, new was better than old, the future was more important than the past, and anything that got in the way of that progress was ruthlessly wiped out.

Such a passing occurred in 1886 when the very last building from the original Fort Collins Military Reservation was torn down. This building was the old officer's quarters. It stood a hundred feet or so from the corner of Linden and Jefferson, toward the river. It was a one story log building that faced Long's Peak, with a little balcony just big enough for one per-

The last military building left from the time of the old fort. This was the officer's quarters. It was torn down in 1888.   Fort Collins Library

son to sit on at the end. This was the house in which the first marriage in Fort Collins was performed in 1866 and the first settler's child was born in 1867. Now that seems like a kind of important building doesn't it?

After the army pulled out in 1866, the building and the lot it sat on was purchased by a private party. Over the years it was used as a residence. Twenty years later it was still standing, but not really in great shape. The owner was resolved to tear it down. The Fort Collins Courier reported this fact on December 30, 1886, reminding everyone that this was the last of the fort buildings. A few days later, the building had been demolished. There was no public outcry to save the building. Most people were glad to see it go since it had become an eyesore. And besides, it had the kiss of death on it . . . it was *old!*

If it is any consolation to you, there is still one building that survives from the time of the fort. It was not one of the military buildings, but rather the little boarding house run by Auntie Stone and built in 1864. Through a series of fortunate events, the building managed to survive into the 20th century when its true value was realized and it was saved. Today it is lovingly preserved at the Fort Collins Museum where people can see it everyday.

Progress And Prohibition.

Even though the economy of northern Colorado was not in the best shape during the last of the 1880s, Fort Collins continued to improve itself and install new luxuries, new conveniences and new city services. 1887 was a very good year for such improvements. One of them was not actually recognized as much of an improvement at the time. This was a development by the newly established agricultural experiment station by the Colorado A and M College. The purpose of this experimental station was to develop new crops that could be grown profitably on the high plains of the Front Range. Well, the college people worked and worked and finally announced that they had perfected the mechanics from growing this ugly looking bulb that they called the Sugar Beet. Nobody noticed this much because not very many people started growing them. It would be a benefit whose time would have to wait. But a couple of other things were very obvious and made 1887 a watershed year for civic improvements.

What made the people of Fort Collins want everything in the world was because it was connected to the rest of the world via the railroad, the telegraph and the newspapers. Almost simultaneously with the introduction of something new, the people of town found out about it and wanted it for themselves, right away. In the summer of 1887, a marvelous new invention, the telephone, rolled into Fort Collins. Now it's true that the system was not very extensive. There was only one line. It connected the city hall on Walnut Street to the water plant on Overland Trail. This was so the fire department could call up and order additional water supplies in the event of a fire. Nevertheless, it was still a telephone and the people of Fort Collins wanted more for themselves. Within six years, the telephone system had expanded to include businesses and residential homes and the first long distance line to Denver and the rest of the world . . . who had no telephones at all. The city was sinfully proud of itself.

Because Fort Collins was a progressive town, its citizens believed in keeping step with the march of progress in all things that promised to aid in its development, and added to the comfort and convenience of the community. In 1887, the people read in the newspaper that the big cities in the country were putting in electricity, so they couldn't understand why they couldn't have electricity too. They didn't even put it to a vote, they just did it.

In October, the city council passed a resolution granting the newly organized Fort Collins Light and Power Company the right to erect poles and wires and all the equipment for transmitting electricity to business and residential areas. The company promised to light up the city by the middle of December. They went to Denver and purchased 10 big arc lights for street lighting. By Christmas of that year, the people of Fort Collins were amazed to see the their downtown come alive with bright lights that turned the night into day. Soon, electric lines were heading off in all directions. The Light and Power company could not keep up with the demand. Everyone wanted power to their house yesterday. This project of wiring every building in town was a huge one. The modern day equivalent would be for the people of today to just rewire every house to hook onto the information superhighway. But the people of Fort Collins took all the progress in stride and never worried about how hard it was to do. That was just the way they were and their community along the Poudre Valley reflected their single-minded march into the future.

At the same time that the City of Fort Collins was bringing new improvements to the town's infrastructure, the citizens of Fort Collins were beginning to insist on the same kind of improvements in the behavior and morals of the people. Fort Collins had been pretty wide open every since the arrival of the railroad and the corresponding arrival of hoards of people. Even while it was happening, powerful forces were gathering to make the town a decent place to live. The social engineering that went on during the 1880s and 1890s was just as significant as the progress being made to build the houses, businesses, streets and turn on the electricity.

The problem was the saloons, and more specifically the liquor. You have to remember that most of the people who came to Fort Collins in the 1880s were solid souls with strong religious beliefs and work ethics. It's true that they had come to the West to make a better life and more money, but that was considered to be a virtue. None of this was compatible to the sorry state of affairs that existed in Fort Collins in 1883. From their point of view, these saloons were unconscionable, all the alcohol was intolerable, the casinos not be endured and they wouldn't even discuss prostitution. It was all the same thing . . . *bad*, and it had to go. Fort Collins was becoming a peaceful, law-abiding little city. Unfortunately, the wild elements of town still remained. Ansel Watrous would write: "The town was full of idle, vicious men, driftwood from railroad and ditch camps, irresponsible creatures without homes or friends who hung around the bars and brothels."

With the election of 1883, a new city council took over after having run on a prohibition platform and promised to end the days of wild living. They passed a new resolution that put a thousand dollar license fee on the saloons. By the end of the year, only six bars remained. Most of the seedier elements of town left for more permissive pastures.

The saloons that remained, many of which were owned by leading citizens, did everything they could to lend an air of respectability to their business. In fact they disguised them as something else. One saloon on Jefferson street was also used for community activities and church socials. Another one on College was called "The Board of Trade," another one had a bowling alley in it, another had a shooting gallery in the basement. All of this concealed what was really happening.

For years the battle raged. Finally, in 1896 a new party of prohibitionists was elected to the city council. They were bolstered in their efforts by the fact that Colorado had given women the right to vote in 1893. Women used their franchise to effect social change. They elected one of these women to the city council, the first woman to serve in that capacity. That council led the way to total prohibition of alcohol in Fort Collins. The saloons were closed at last. Fort Collins went dry and stayed dry until 1970.

But the good people of Fort Collins were not going to wait all those years before alcohol was banned to start other elements of social change. During the years of the great expansion, the people built several churches, organized new school districts and founded any number of civic organizations like the Odd fellows, Masons and Knights of Columbus. The Ladies Auxiliary of the Ku Klux Klan sold baked goods and conducted bazaars to raise money for the needy.

Fort Collins' Only Lynching.

By 1888, Fort Collins was settling down to respectability.
There was electricity and running water in most of the houses.
Gone were the days of the wild and woolly frontier town.
Gone were most of the saloons, the brothels, the gambling
halls and the riff-raff that all this attracted. No more was the
civil and moral code of the community held in open defiance.

Many of the pioneers were from the best blood of the eastern states. They had grown up in a society in which the courts
were in full swing, where human life was protected by strin-
gent laws, where property rights were respected, and where
compliance to constituted authority was a prerequisite to good
citizenship. The people knew that lawless acts were frequently
the case on the border, but restrained their desires for
vengeance, hated the idea of mob rule and were content to let
the law take its course. But it didn't happen that way once.
Something happened that so enraged these peaceful people
that their thin veneer of civilization was peeled away like an
apple.

Eva and James Howe lived in a little house on Walnut
Street, just a half block from Linden Street where Old Town
Square is today. They had a five-year-old daughter. James
Howe was a millwright and a very good mechanic and was
well respected in the business community. Eva Howe was a
happy, pleasant woman . . . quite pretty, and very much liked
by all the other ladies. Most of the time, the Howes lived quietly as the 1880s rolled by.

But alcohol was eating at James Howe. As the disease progressed in him, he was less and less in control of himself and
he drank more everyday. When James Howe got drunk, he
got mean. The more he drank, the meaner he got, and he took
it all out on his wife Eva. He started to beat and mistreat her.
She would beg for James to stop drinking, but he never did.
As the situation went from bad to worse, Eva began to think
about leaving him. Then one night in the spring of 1888,
Howe came home from the saloon and shamefully abused and
beat his wife. He also threatened to kill her before he passed
out. That was the last straw for Eva. She made up her mind
that she was going to take their daughter and go home to
Canada.

The next morning, April 4th, Eva pleaded with Howe not to go out to the saloon again, but he wouldn't listen and left. Fearing for her safety, Eva quickly began packing. She did not expect her husband to return until late that night, and she was resolved to be gone before then. But Howe came home unexpectedly at noon and caught her packing. A terrific fight ensued. Howe raged and ranted and drunkenly repeated his threat to kill his wife. He pulled out his knife and staggered toward her. Eva ran from the house in terror with Howe in hot pursuit. He caught her in front of the house, on Walnut Street in Old Town, and in full view of several horrified witnesses, slashed her face with the knife. Then he struck again and this blow sliced her throat and severed her jugular vein. Eva fell to her hands and knees with Howe on her back stabbing and slashing. She struggled to her feet, staggered down the street, crying "Murder!" Then she fell on her face and died. The murderer stood over her body and said, "You can't leave me. I'll kill you first." But the deed was already done. Young Eva Howe had breathed her last.

Bystanders on the street stood rooted to their spots. They could not believe what they had seen. James Howe staggered back into the cottage before any of them moved. Then they all moved at once to Eva Howe's body. Seeing that she was already dead, several of the men in the rapidly growing crowd went into the house and found Howe laying down on the only bed. The couple's five year old daughter was cringing in the corner and sobbing.

Howe was taken into custody by the men just as the deputy sheriff arrived. With the help of several men, the deputy marched Howe the three blocks to the county jail. The jail was a new building on courthouse square just where the Sheriff's Office is today. As they rushed along the crowd got bigger and uglier. By the time they got there, the crowd was very excited and threats were shouted as Howe was locked in a cell.

During the afternoon Fort Collins was paralyzed by the brutal killing. It had happened at one o'clock in the afternoon and for the balance of the day, business was completely shut down. The news spread like wildfire through all 2,000 people in town. Soon the news had spread to the whole county, and many people came into town to hear the whole story told over and over again. Tension rose and everywhere little groups of men, woman and children spoke in bated breath.

Late that afternoon, a coroners jury was convened and when they came out they made the following statement: "We the jurors, do say that Eva Howes met her death this 4th of April, 1888 from the effect of many stab wounds from a knife in the hands of her husband James H. Howe." So it was official. There was no doubt now in the minds of the people of the Poudre Valley what the facts were in this killing. They were startled by its unprovoked brutality. Things like this did not happen here, not anymore. It was intolerable.

By nightfall, the streets downtown were still full of people. Small groups formed and reformed under the light of the street lamps and spoke in whispers. There was no public gathering, no town meeting, no leaders on stumps screaming for justice. It was deathly quiet.

At precisely 8 o'clock that night, the lights in Fort Collins suddenly went out . . . all the lights in the whole town. It was pitch black. At the jail house the deputy and his assistants sat in the dark and sweated. Soon they heard the sound of many feet coming down the street and from the dark and large crowd of men suddenly appeared around the jail. Many of them wore masks. They beat at the door of the jail and broke it down. The deputies were all placed under guard. Not a word was spoken. Then the men used a hammer and chisel on the iron door leading to the cell block. It flew open. The mob went down the hallway and stood before the cell that held a terrified James Howe. With the same hammer and chisel, the door to the cell was broken open and Howe was in the hands of the mob.

Howe screamed for mercy as he was led out of the building. He begged the mob to spare him. No own spoke to him. Nobody said anything. Howe was held by many men and led to a construction derrick where a rope had already been thrown over the cross bar. The noose was placed around Howe's neck. Then with a mighty heave by a score of men, Howe shot up into the air like a rocket. It was soon over. The crowd dispersed, the lights went back on and Fort Collins went on about its business.

The next day, a second coroner's jury was convened and announced that the body of James Howe had been found hanging at court house square . . . dead at the hands of an infuriated and unknown mob. And that was it. It was Fort Collins' only lynching.

On the day before this incident, the people of Fort Collins had gone to the polls to vote on a new addition to their sewer system. To all outward appearances, the town had become a law-abiding, church-going, and sensible community. Now there was this. Maybe the reason the city reacted so violently was because they thought they were better than that. Or maybe it was the crime itself. Women really were regarded in those days as the weaker sex and were often revered by their men. You certainly did not kill them. You did not stab them to death in front of your house in the presence of a group of people. From their point of view, justice had been served and townspeople went on with the rest of their lives.

Struggling Toward The 20th Century.

Throughout all of the years in the final two decades of the century, northern Colorado was increasingly affected by the national economy and events around the world. In fact, it was economics that really set the tone for the lives of the Poudre Valley pioneers.

After the Civil War, America embarked on a huge period of expansion with the country leading the world in agricultural production. Larimer County benefited with the introduction of many advances in agricultural technology that included the disc harrow, the corn-shucker and the biggest improvement of them all, the giant combine harvester. But the bubble was about to break.

In the heady years following the arrival of the railroad in 1877, Fort Collins and Larimer County were realizing part of the potential that the Poudre Valley had always possessed. By 1883, the population of the city had increased from just a few hundred to over 2,000. Population growth in the county had been even greater. During this time more buildings had been constructed, more homes built, more businesses started and more farms established than at any other time in our history. But every boom has a bust.

The principal reason why the steam went out of the boom was because the farmers and ranchers were not doing well.

Fort Collins in 1899. The tall building right of center was the new Larimer County courthouse. Only about half of Franklin Avery's original city plan had been developed.

The main money crop was wheat and the price of wheat, nationally, was going down. Alfalfa was a glut on the market, and the farmers couldn't sell it at any price. Plus they had not done a very good job of rotating their crops and replenishing the soil, so the yield per acre went down a lot. Many of the farmers were in debt for their land and had loans on improvements, equipment and the like, so they were just barely getting by. What's more the ranchers were also feeling the pinch. Beginning in 1885, the value of cattle and horses began to plummet. It's an old truism that in an agricultural area, unless the producers thrive, the town cannot prosper. Well, that's what happened. Before long the whole area was in an economic funk. There were many bankruptcies and quite a few people just gave up and moved on. Between 1883 and 1890, the population of Fort Collins only increased by 42 people.

By 1889, things were getting down to bedrock and there were no more notches to tighten in the belt. The agricultural community was looking for something . . . anything, that would lead them out of the economic swamp. As it turned out, fortune would come from the last place that anybody expected. Moreover, nobody was very happy with the solution.

The chances are you have heard about the huge range wars

that raged in the West between cattlemen and sheep ranchers. Well, it was a terrible confrontation. The cattlemen said that the sheep grazed the grass down so short that the cows starved to death, and that was true. The open spaces of Larimer County was cattle country. It had always been cattle country and they expected it to always remain cattle country. But times were hard. So in desperation, a few brave souls held their breath and staked their future to a bunch of little . . . fluffy . . . white lambs.

In the winter of 1889 they brought in 3,500 Mexican lambs to be fattened up for the Chicago market on the very same hay, corn and wheat that the farmers couldn't give away. When the spring of 1890 came, the lambs were shipped off and sold for wonderful profits. Violá! A new industry was born. Soon everybody was on the bandwagon and feeding sheep.

How good was the new industry? Well, by 1896, the Poudre Valley was ringing to the sound of bahs and bleats. The number of lambs being fed had gone from 3,500 to 200,000. By the turn of the century, the number would grow to 400,000 lambs and Larimer County became the lamb feeding capital of the country. Now the farmers had a ready, home grown market for all the hay and wheat it could grow, and soon the bust of a few years before was just a memory.

There was another development that also would contribute heavily to the new economic renaissance. Remember back in 1888, that the agricultural experimental station for Colorado A and M College had developed the technique for growing sugar beets? Well, in 1898 the Spanish American War broke out and suddenly the supply of cane sugar was no longer coming in from Cuba. It didn't take the farmers very long to figure out that this would become a new industry that would make the economy even better.

So Fort Collins went racing toward the end of the century and was poised for greatness. In the final decade, the population of the city went from 2,000 to over 3,000 people. They were a confident bunch and with good reason because the coming of the 20th century would spell the greatest period of prosperity and growth that Fort Collins had ever known.

For now, the people had a chance to pause with the passing of the 19th century and reflect on all that had happened. In less than 40 years, Fort Collins had grown from a lonely military post, way out on the frontier, 600 miles from the boundaries of civilized rule, to a city with schools, churches, theaters, fraternal organizations, parks and thriving business enterprises. They had accomplished more than anyone had a right to expect. But they believed in their future, fought to secure it and never looked back.

I suppose that's a pretty good definition of what a Boom Town actually is . . . ups and down, highs and lows, heartaches and jubilation on the road to tomorrow and a better vision along the Poudre Valley.

Part V

"Diamonds In The Rough" 1900-1933

T HE 20TH CENTURY . . . *Never had Americans felt more confident, more vigorous, more eager to assert themselves. In 1900, the United States was the world's largest industrial power. The nation had nearly half the world's railroad mileage, shipped half its freight, pumped half its oil, forged a third of its steel, and mined a third of its gold. Remarkable new inventions — the automobile, the electric light bulb and the telephone, to name just three — were transforming the way people lived. There were now 45 states. The entire country was getting bigger, stronger, and seemingly more wonderful.*

From, "Our Glorious Century"

The turn of the century for Fort Collins. This is a picture of downtown, looking north along Linden Street. Today, it's Old Town Square. Fort Collins Library

Roaring Into A New Era.

The year was 1900, the turn of the century. This momentous occasion was greeted with more than the usual amount of celebration. All over the world, people were talking about the arrival of the 20th century and what it would mean to each of them in their lives.

In the Poudre Valley, the year 1900 found the citizens feeling pretty good about themselves. The whole area was prosperous and economically healthy. People considered themselves to be progressive and in tune with the times. They certainly did not think that just because they were farther away from the centers of population and commerce that they were any less far-sighted.

In good times, people are much more willing to chase the tail of progress and pay for new and better services for their city. It was also a sign of the times. A new century always brings out the best in entrepreneurial enterprise. The people reasoned that the start of a new century must mean the beginning of a new age. So even if there wasn't a new age, the people created one so they wouldn't be disappointed.

In fact, Fort Collins and Larimer County had a lot going for them with the arrival of the new century and they carried that inertia with them right into early years of the 1900s. The decade between 1900 and 1910 produced the most prosperous era in the history of the city to that time. It was not exactly a boom, just a steady and substantial growth in all areas of business in the area. In those ten years, the population of Fort Collins increased from 3,153 to 8210 people, and the population of the county more than doubled from 12,000 to over 25,000 people.

B.F. Hottel. As a young man, he came with the railroad and became Fort Collins' first millionaire as president of the Great Western Sugar Beet plant of Fort Collins.

Fort Collins Library

The engine that was driving all this growth was the explosion of the lamb feeding and wool growing industry. By 1901, Larimer County was feeding over 400,000 lambs annually. This made it the number one center for this business in the whole country. It had such a huge impact on the town, that Fort Collins High School adopted the Lambkin as a mascot, much to the chagrin of generations of future graduates.

Right on the heels of livestock came the state-wide industry of growing sugar beets. These had become the answer to the dwindling sugar supplies during the Spanish-American War that began in 1898 and shut off the supply of sugar cane from Cuba. So great was the demand for sugar that various groups began to lobby for the construction of sugar beet plants to process the crops. Loveland was the first town in the county to get a sugar beet plant that was completed in 1901. Fort Collins was right behind with a plan of its own. In 1903, a local consortium, led by a man named Benjamin Hottel, raised over a million dollars to build a sugar beet plant on Vine Drive, east of College Avenue.

Visions Along The Poudre Valley

B.F. Hottel came to Fort Collins with the railroad in 1877 and was a successful businessman in town. He ended up being the city's first self-made millionaire. Hottel put up the lion's share of the money to build the sugar beet plant in Fort Collins. The plant cost 1.25 million dollars to build and was, by far, the biggest commercial enterprise ever undertaken to that date by the community. Hottel took the helm as first president of the company.

By 1904, the sugar beet plant was processing 15 million pounds of granulated sugar a year. By 1910, the plant had put nearly 8 million dollars into the Larimer County economy in wages and purchase of sugar beets from the farmers. These days that doesn't sound like a lot of money, but think of it in proportion to the economy of the day. In 1900 the average weekly wage for a man was ten dollars, a loaf of bread was a nickel and the very same sugar sold for four cents a pound. So to get an idea of what money was really worth in those days, you have to multiply by a factor of at least ten to one.

Nevertheless, the one-two punch of the powerful sugar beet industry and the equally muscular lamb-feeding and wool

A German-Russian immigrant family in 1904. They came to the Poudre Valley to work in the sugar beet fields. Fort Collins Library

The Fort Collins sugar beet plant, built in 1903, with a trolley headed by on the way to Lindenmeier Lake.

growing concerns was dragging all the rest of the business community with it. Fort Collins was looking like a pretty solid town.

Consistent with such a time, the good citizens of Fort Collins, in cahoots with their hard charging city government, began a new round of civic improvements. They rolled out a program of community projects whose benefits are still being enjoyed today. It was an extensive list that literally touched every person, group or circumstance in town. By the time that the sugar beet plant was finished and operating in 1903, the overall city plan was getting clearer.

Always first was water. Lesson number one for living in the Poudre Valley was to make sure that the water supply and its delivery system was secure. People never forgot that this is a semi-arid area with less than 15 inches of moisture annually. Next, in "improvement importance" was gas for home heating, a better library, a hospital, youth recreation facilities, street paving, a city park and mass transit. All of that was going to cost real money.

Undaunted the city got moving. It laid out a plan to upgrade the original water system that had been built in 1886. The town was growing so fast that the system was totally inadequate. The voters approved a bond issue that would pay the $150,000 the new system was going to cost. The work continued through 1903 and the first part of 1904. The system was of considerable size. The specifications called for it to deliver 4 million gallons of water a day to the city with a water pressure of 90 pounds per square inch at the intersection of Laporte and College.

It was very hard work. The winter of 1903 had been just awful. It seemed to snow all the time, one storm after another. You couldn't even get into the mountains because they were drifted shut with all the snow they were getting. Then in April of 1904, the weather turned warm and pleasant. This was more like it and the work on the water system progressed at a brisk pace. Most of the work was finished by the middle of May. The city fathers inspected, and all agreed that now everybody would soon have all the water they needed.

Nobody really bothered to worry that the warm weather was making the river run fast and high. Oh well, it was spring and the river was supposed to be high. But then great storm clouds appeared over the mountains and it was clear that it was raining in the high country, a drenching torrential rain.

The Old Man And His City.

The Colorado and Southern Railroad train labored to a stop amidst clouds of steam and a rattling of cars at the station in Fort Collins, Colorado. It was a bright spring day in May, 1904.

A young, well-dressed man stepped off the train and looked about. A short distance down the platform stood an elderly gentleman. His face was seamed with the lines of many years and he leaned slightly on a cane. The newcomer crossed the platform and spoke to the old man.

The Fort Collins C&S railroad depot, in the center of Laporte Avenue, just off College Ave., in 1904. Fort Collins Library

"Are you Mr. Benjamin Whedbee", he asked?

"That I am, Lad," answered the old man, "You look like your father."

"It was very kind of you to meet me, sir," said the newcomer.

"Think nothing of it," said Whedbee, shaking hands. "I'm always glad to welcome new folks to town. Especially when he's the son of an old friend. Now come along and we'll get you into a room at the Tedmon House."

The newcomer picked up his bag and followed Whedbee to the front of the station where a surprisingly elegant carriage was waiting.

"Climb aboard, son," said Whedbee, "next stop, the best hotel north of Denver!" The carriage rolled away from the station and onto Laporte street. The hooves of the horse stirred up little clouds of dust as it plodded along. The carriage crossed College Avenue and turned down Walnut Street. As they passed pedestrians on the street, everyone seemed to turn and speak a greeting to the old man.

"Howdy, Mr. Whedbee, how you feeling today?"

"Mornin', Uncle Ben, lovely day don't you think?"

Benjamin Whedbee smiled at all and greeted them with a wave of his hand.

"You seem to know everybody, Mr. Whedbee," said the newcomer.

"I used to," nodded Whedbee, "but so many new folks have come to town in the last few years that I kinda lose track. There must be four thousand people in Fort Collins nowadays."

Benjamin Whedbee, Fort Collins' first mayor. He was known to everyone as Uncle "Ben".
Fort Collins Library

"When did you come to Fort Collins?" asked the young man.

"1863," said Whedbee, "It was upstream of the river a few miles, near Laporte. Prettiest place you ever saw. I called it Pleasant Valley. There wasn't any of this here then. The army didn't move the fort till after the flood in '64 washed 'em out. Then they moved here where the city is today. Been lots of changes."

"What's this building over here?" asked the newcomer.

"That's our city hall and fire station," answered Whedbee, "finished in 1888." The young man looked at the handsome two-story brick building. It was made of red brick and was crowned with an elegant tower where a bell hung to sound the alarm whenever there was a fire.

The carriage made a left turn at the intersection of Walnut and Linden Streets. On the northwest corner stood a massive structure.

"That's the Poudre Valley Bank," observed Whedbee. "It was built back in 1882 by Bill Stover and Charlie Sheldon. Quite a building. It cost them $32,000. They brought the vault in from Denver. You should see inside. They have two teller windows — with six lights of plate glass set in the railing with brass wickets. They went all out."

The building look like a bank, even without the big carved sign that said, 'BANK', right under the cupola that sat atop the third floor.

As the carriage reached the end of Linden Street where it intersected with Jefferson, the young man could see the Tedmon House on the corner across Jefferson. It was a beautiful building. Built in 1880 by

The Tedmon House was built in 1880. It was northern Colorado's finest hotel, advertising that it had a bathroom on every floor.   Fort Collins Library

Bolivar Tedmon and his wife, the hotel was a three story structure with 65 rooms. The carriage that had brought them there from the train station belonged to the hotel and was provided for the comfort of the guests. The young man helped Benjamin Whedbee down from the carriage and they went inside.

On the first floor, beyond the registration desk, was a baggage room, barber shop, sample room for traveling salesmen, a dining room with two chandeliers and the kitchen. Brussels carpets covered the stairways and halls.

After the newcomer had checked in and taken his suitcase to his room, he returned to the lobby. Whedbee disengaged

The Miller Block. Built by Frank Miller Sr. It was a bar, and a house goods store, called "The Fair". It had a two-story outhouse that was not torn down until 1948.

himself from the conversation he had been having with the desk clerk and joined the young man.

"I told the clerk I wanted to give you a little tour around town and he's gonna let me use the hotel's carriage. I'm not as spry as I was once, so you can ride in style. Besides, the town's gettin' so big you can't just walk across it in five minutes like you used to."

As the two were leaving the hotel, the young man remarked that there was a drug store in the building with Stover's name on it.

"Yeah, the Stover's are into everything around here, banks, cattle, farming and this drug store. He even has one of those new telephone machines that he's got hooked up to his house on Willow. I suppose soon that our city will be traversed by a bewildering maze of those wires."

The two climbed back into the carriage. The newcomer had to carefully help Whedbee get aboard.

"If you don't mind me asking, sir," asked the man, "how old are you?"

"92 years old . . . this year. Let's go."

The carriage crossed Jefferson and went back down Linden

Street. When they had passed by the Poudre Valley Bank and waited while a team of mules had pulled a huge wagon filled with sugar beets down Walnut street, Whedbee pointed to the building sitting on the corner diagonal from the bank.

"That's the Miller Block," he said. The Miller Block was a solid looking sandstone building with two stories. In the middle of the building was an ornate, carved stone slab, set at the top of the top of the building. It said, "F. Miller Block, 1888."

Whedbee's eyes twinkled as he said, "Frank didn't really finish the building until 1891. Guess it doesn't matter very much, nobody will ever know the difference anyway. It used to be a saloon down there at the other end of the building where the department store is now. But we passed prohibition for the town in 1896, and old Frank had to close up. He used to call his place the 'Sample Room'. I don't know who he thought he was kidding. But that the building cost him $30,000 to build. You know it has a two-story brick outhouse? Only one in town."

The horse clip-clopped its way south on Linden Street toward Mountain Avenue. At the end of Linden, on the corner of Mountain, was a stunning red stone building with carved columns and a central archway over the entrance.

"This is Franklin Avery's First National Bank," said Whedbee. "Years ago, Franklin was in business with Stover and Sheldon at Poudre Valley Bank, but he broke off and formed his own bank about 25 years ago. Those fellows have been going at it, hot and heavy, ever since. Every time one of them would build a new bank building, the other one had to top it. This is Franklin's new bank. He got Montezuma Fuller to design it for him and built it seven years ago in 1897. It's a beauty. Sometimes I think we wouldn't have so many nice buildings if those fellows hadn't been so competitive."

"These buildings are so solid," said the young man, "Where did all the stone come from to build them?"

"Lucky thing about that," answered Uncle Ben, "those mountains over there give us all the stone we need. High quality stuff, too. See that funny shaped mountain?" He pointed to the West. "We call that Horsetooth Mountain because the rocks at the top are shaped like teeth. In the valley below there's a little settlement called Stout. There's a quarry there. They don't take as much out as they used to, but a few years ago the rail-

Downtown Fort Collins, 1904. There was a drinking fountain for horses in the middle of the intersection of College and Mountain Avenues, supplied by the underground river that flows beneath the streets. Fort Collins Library

road had over a thousand men working up there. They took out red, white and gray sandstone, granite and marble. Shipped it all over the country. We had the materials close at hand, so we built all these buildings and our homes with native rock. It ought to last for a long time. We aren't just building a town the easiest way we can, son. There's a future here. Sooner than you think Fort Collins is going to be a city that people know about. We're modern! Hell, this is 1904!"

As the carriage with the two men turned west on Mountain Avenue, Whedbee stopped the horse in the middle of the intersection with College Avenue. There was a large red sandstone water fountain there and Whedbee let the horse drink. He turned in the seat and pointed back at the old wooden building on the corner.

"That was my mercantile store. Built it in 1873," he said. "It seemed like a good place for a store. I figured that most of the growth would be in this direction. Unfortunately, some of the early settlers who had built businesses in the old part of town thought that this would hurt their property values. It's been a sore point in town for thirty years. I've no idea how it'll turn out. Maybe someday they'll tear down my old store and put up something else."

Whedbee gave the reins a snap and the carriage moved off

down Mountain Avenue to the West. As they approached
Mason Street and the end of the next block, the old man
pointed out an old cabin-like structure near the corner. The
building seemed out of place and dilapidated among all the
modern buildings the young man had seen. On the front of
the cabin was a sign that said, "Paint Shop".

"That cabin was Auntie Stone's place," said Whedbee. "It
used to be the mess hall for the officers at the fort back in '65.
Later Auntie Stone used it for a boarding house. But she died a
few years ago, and the cabin hasn't been of much use since.
There's been talk that it'll be torn down soon. Shame. I think
it's about the only building left from the time of the old fort.
We oughta save it."

The horse stepped over the railroad tracks in the intersection of Mason and Mountain and continued west. It was clear
to the young man that they had entered the residential section
of the town. There were homes and trees lining the street on
both sides of Mountain Avenue, which was a wide street
indeed.

"Why are all the streets so wide here," asked the newcomer?

"Franklin Avery's idea," replied the old man. "He was a
surveyor by trade before he came here and got rich in banking.
He helped do the platting for the Greeley Colony. Then he
came over here in 1871
and laid out the streets for
the city. He said that
there was plenty of space
to use and that he was
going to use it. The idea
was that he wanted the
streets to be wide enough
so you could turn a team
of horses and a wagon
around without having to
back up. Speaking of
Franklin Avery, his house
is just up ahead."

The Avery House was built in 1879. It was the home
of three generations of the Avery family. Today it has
been restored, on the list of historical landmarks and
open to the public.   Fort Collins Library

They sat quietly as the carriage rolled along another two
blocks west on Mountain. Then Whedbee pulled up on the
right to a large two-story home constructed of stone that was

of several colors. There were many dormers and gables to the house and there was a large stone porch in front. The home gave the impression of a sturdy residence, built for the ages.

On the porch sat a man and a woman. Whedbee waved and called to them. "Afternoon, Franklin," he said, "How are you and Sarah doing today?"

"Good afternoon, Uncle Ben," answered Sarah Avery. "What's the occasion?"

"I'm giving this young fella a tour of our town. He just came in on the morning train. His father's a friend of mine."

"Say Benjamin," said Franklin Avery, "I want to talk to you about your building there at the corner of College and Mountain."

"What about it?" answered Whedbee.

"I was thinking that it might be just the place for a new bank building," said Avery.

Uncle Ben just shook his head, popped the reins of the horse and muttered to the newcomer, "Man just doesn't know when to quit. That bank building he has isn't ten years old yet and already he thinks he ought to build another one."

"Bye," he shouted out loud, "Gotta be movin' on. I'll talk to you about that some other time."

The Averys waved good-bye, and the carriage pulled away. Whedbee turned south on Meldrum Street. The street was a dusty, unpaved, rutted thoroughfare. The few homes on the street were modest and small. It was clear that they were reaching the end of the main part of town, rural farms dotted the landscape to the west and south. The old man went just a block and turned left on Oak street and they proceeded to the east, back toward College Avenue.

"Just one more stop," said Whedbee. "I want you to meet our mayor." "Who's that?" asked the young man.

"Name's Doc P.J. McHugh. He lives in the castle down the street there." They crossed College Avenue and went one more block east. Standing on the corner of Oak and Remington Streets was a large, three-story home that did, indeed, look like a castle. It was the home of Doctor McHugh who was in his second year as mayor of Fort Collins. It was constructed of the, now familiar, red sandstone and there was a turret-like tower that rose to the roof line in front. Behind the home was a large carriage house that Doctor McHugh had converted to

Fort Collins' first hospital. Benjamin Whedbee pulled up in front of the house and the young man helped him dismount.

"Gotta see the Doc about this arthritis," he grumbled. "Come on along, I'll introduce you."

Doctor McHugh met them at the front door. "Afternoon, Benjamin," he said. "How are we feeling today?"

"I'm an old man," snapped Whedbee, "Whaddya expect."

"Well, come on in and let me take a look," answered the doctor. "Who's your friend?"

Introduction completed, Whedbee turned to the newcomer and said, "I hope you enjoyed our little turn around town."

"Very much," said the young man. "I'm sure I'm going to love it here."

"Well, you'd better," said Whedbee. "We have the

The house of the mayors. Built in 1885 by Dr. P.J. McHugh. He used the carriage house behind as the city's first hospital. The home has been restored as a business on the corner of Oak and Remington. Fort Collins Library

best little town you ever saw here in Fort Collins. We're progressive. Why we have a university, a sugar beet plant and the best farmland in the world here. Lots of opportunities for a young fella to make a name for himself."

"I'll try, sir," said the newcomer.

"Why don't you take the carriage back to the hotel yourself," said Uncle Ben. "I've got some business to discuss with his honor here. If you get lost just ask anybody. Good Luck."

"Thank you for your kindness, Mr. Whedbee," said the young man, "I'll be seeing you again real soon."

"Good enough," said Whedbee, "Better hurry along now. It looks like it might rain."

The young newcomer returned the carriage to the Tedmon Hotel, but he disappeared and his whereabouts thereafter are unknown.

History tells us that Benjamin Whedbee was Fort Collins' first mayor, 1873-79. He died in October, 1910 at the age of 98.

The Poudre Valley Bank became the Linden Hotel and served as a hotel for many years. It was completely restored in 1994. The building is on the list of historical landmarks.

The "House of the Mayors", once owned by Dr. P.J. McHugh has been beautifully restored and is now a private business . . . a fly fishing shop.

Franklin Avery purchased the Whedbee building at the corner of College and Mountain where he erected a magnificent, white marble building for his First National Bank in 1909. It was demolished in 1963 and Columbia Savings built a smaller building on the corner.

Just as Ben Whedbee had predicted, the following day, May 20, 1904, it did rain and Fort Collins was hit by the most destructive flood of the Poudre River in history.

Fort Collins' Most Destructive Flood.

Early on the morning of May 20, 1904, the storm that had been raging over the mountains, spread to the lands along the Front Range. It rained in buckets! No longer was this just a welcome spring soaking, the rains in the mountains were melting that big snowpack, and the people began casting worried eyes on the dark river in the gloom before dawn. They could

The 1904 flood. Pictured is Linden Street with the bridge and the railroad washed away.   Fort Collins Library

not see it, but they could hear it. The sound was a deafening roar that rumbled through the dark.

With the coming of the light of day, the size of the danger became all to apparent. The river was a raging torrent, running bank high and faster than a horse could run. It was rising at the rate of a foot an hour and already it was spilling out of its banks and over the rich farm lands. The water spilled into the network of irrigation ditches and made sudden rivers of them all, equally as dangerous as their boiling parent.

Quickly the people mobilized for action. There was no immediate worry for the main city of Fort Collins itself, even though this flood gave every indication of being as big, or bigger, than the one that had washed away the army camp in Laporte in 1864. Everyone remembered that the result of that flood had been to move the Army camp to higher ground and thereby establish the military fort that became the city. It was just as well that the city was on higher ground, because, just as in 1864, there wasn't a thing they could do about it. But Fort Collins was not just some little military fort anymore. It was now a town of about 6,000 people with hundreds and hundreds of homes, farms, buildings and commercial enterprises clustered on both sides of the river, up and downstream.

The Poudre River became a raging torrent in this photograph from the morning of May 20, 1904.

Throughout the afternoon of May 20th, the river continued to rise. The crest was going to peak at 14 feet above flood stage. The river surged out of its banks and turned the north end of the city into a lake. Thousands of acres of prime agricultural land was laid waste. Every bridge on the river from the mouth of the canyon to Greeley was washed away in the deluge, dozens of watergates in the big irrigation ditches were swept away. All of Bellvue, Laporte and even Wellington was underwater. 150 homes and buildings in Fort Collins were pushed along by the raging water and smashed to pieces like match sticks. There was no time to sound the alarm, no time to get out of its way. The wall of water was upon them with little or no warning. Hundreds of people were stranded, and the dark muddy water was relentlessly destroying every man-made thing in its path, and worst of all, on the other side of the river, down in the flood plain, was the brand new, million dollar plus, economic engine of Fort Collins . . . the sugar beet plant.

Throughout the afternoon, B.F. Hottel, president of the Great Western Sugar Beet Plant in Fort Collins, watched the waters of the Cache La Poudre river rise. With each new crest the water surged closer and closer to the plant. Inside, a gang of men were furiously filling sandbags and stacking them around the 10 millions pounds of processed granulated sugar that was stored in the plant. Already water was pouring into the north side of the building and it was starting to get dark.

At 7 p.m. on that Friday night, the crest of the flood passed, and the waters finally began to drain away. The sand-bagging operation had been a success. Even though there was a foot and half of water in the plant. The stored sugar was saved. It was a terrible mess and there was two feet of mud to haul away, but the plant, the sugar and most of the equipment was saved. Everyone breathed a huge sigh of relief. However, the crest of the flood was still rolling downstream and tragedy was waiting just around the bend of the river. Downstream from the center of Fort Collins, on the far east end of today's Horsetooth Road, was the two story cabin of George Strauss.

George Strauss was one of the real Fort Collins pioneers. He had come to the valley in 1860. He had seen at least four big floods of the river in his time, and he was not shy about getting out of their way. But Strauss was old and feeble, in his 70s in 1904, and the surging water was just to much for him. He was swept along by the river and pinned against a fence where he hung on all night long and was found, barely alive, the next morning by a neighbor. Strauss had survived the flood, but the cold and the wet had given him pneumonia. He died the next day. He was the only fatality of the flood.

When the people of Fort Collins counted up all their losses, they amounted to over a million dollars, as much as it had cost to build the sugar beet plant. 150 homes were gone. Thousands of acres of prime farm land was flooded and destroyed. It was the worst and most destructive flood in our history. Curiously, George Strauss' cabin survived the deluge. You can see the cabin today. It is preserved at the far east end of Horsetooth Road, right next to the river. You can walk all around the area and read the whole story on the information signs. Maybe when you do, you will be able to close your eyes and hear the raging river in your mind.

Before We Were So Rudely Interrupted!

The flood of 1904 was a terrifying experience for the City of Fort Collins. But on the whole, the town had been lucky. Most of the city had no flood damage. With the economy being as strong as it was, the people were able to lick their wounds, rebuild and continue to march. The flood was frightening, expensive and very inconvenient. However, you get the feeling that it was regarded as just another hurdle to cross. The city was not going to give up on all the improvements they had planned, nor were they going to give up their vision of being the most progressive and modern city that anyone could imagine. And they could imagine quite a bit.

After it was all over, the people of Fort Collins had to laugh about the flood of the river coming, almost to the day, with the completion of the new water system that was supposed to make sure that everyone had enough water to live day by day. However, the river itself soon returned to normal and

Built with Carnegie and city money in 1910, the public library is now the Fort Collins museum.

Fort Collins Library

it was not long at all before everyone was very happy that they had installed the system.

Other projects were also initiated in 1904. In that same year the city spent $15,000 building a new Carnegie Library in Lincoln Park. Today it is still called Library Park, and the library building has become the Fort Collins Museum.

A second project that year was even more ambitious. B.F. Hottel, never known for letting the grass grow under his feet and a man who took life in big hunks, decided that it was time for the city to have a gas company. He spent $100,000 to establish the Poudre Valley Gas Company to put gas into everyone's home and business for heating. Hottel thought that a gas company would be good for the city in the same manner in which he thought the sugar beet plant would be good for the city. The fact that he got rich in the process was something he considered to be only secondary.

There were other projects underway in the community as well. In 1906, the hospital association got organized and then built a hospital. Before this time the hospital was mostly at your house and the doctor came there. The association changed that when they built a large brick building at the corner of Mathews and Magnolia, which is still in use today.

Also the needs of young people and their proper upbringing was not ignored. The families in town regarded the raising of children as being, one, the responsibility of everyone, and, two, much too important to be left to chance. They reasoned, accurately enough, that all the kids should be given a place to

The citizens of the city raised $90,000 in volunteer contributions to build a youth center, Y.M.C.A. Today the building is the Elk's Lodge at the corner of Oak and Remington. Fort Collins Library

gather and blow off steam as was natural for growing children and that this place ought to be supervised by responsible adults. Sort of on the principle of "Putting all your eggs into one basket and then watching that basket."

So the community began a volunteer fund-raising project to build a Y.M.C.A. The building was built at the corner of Remington and Oak. Years later it became the Elk's Lodge and remains so today. In just a few months they had raised $90,000 in volunteer contributions, and the center was built. I have no idea where they got all the money to do this. Today a center like that would cost millions and millions of dollars and would be spread out over our entire population. In 1906, they only had 6,000 in Fort Collins, and they did it anyway.

The following year, 1907, the city decided that it needed a nice, new city park. So they went out in the country, west of town, and paid $48,000 to buy John Sheldon's 60 acre farm. The city workers vowed they would make it the most beautiful park anywhere. Today the fruits of all that labor can be seen any day at City Park, with the great big trees, open areas of grass and lawn, and ducks and geese swimming around on Sheldon Lake just off west Mulberry. Fireworks are still fired off over the lake every year on the 4th of July.

Well, the park was just what people wanted and they

Everyone liked to go to the city park. Until the 1950s, you did your swimming in Sheldon Lake. There was also boating and picnicking.   Fort Collins Library

liked going there for picnics. What they didn't like was how far away it was. In fact, they didn't really like how far away everything was. The city was now quite large, 2.1 square miles. The automobile was still a scarce commodity. Most of the people still used a horse and buggy or they walked where they wanted to go. They began to clamor for something better. The city, always ready to be accommodating, obliged the people by giving them rapid transit. In 1907, they began construction on the Fort Collins Municipal Interurban Railway System, the trolley cars. The city's plan was to have it finished by the end of the year. They worked on the system all summer long.

The system was initially five miles of track. It went all over downtown, south on College Avenue to Pitkin, east to Whedbee and then back to downtown. It also went down Mountain Avenue to near City Park. As the city grew, the line went all the way out to Lindenmeier Lake. The trolleys were

 set up to run down the middle of the streets. That's why there are large medians on College and Mountain Avenue. The work was finished in December and on New Year's Eve, 1907, the little electric trolley cars, the same one that

The trolley system was an easy way to get where you were going in Fort Collins. The trolleys were installed in 1907 and operated until 1951. Fort Collins Library

runs down Mountain Avenue today during the summer, went into operation and gave service to the whole town every 20 minutes.

The Fort Collins trolley system was the neatest thing you ever saw. The little trolley cars were colorful, dependable and fun. For the most part, they really served the majority of the community for many years. However, in the end, the trolleys were taken out of service and the tracks paved over. But then, that's another story.

Enter The Union Pacific.

The trolley was not the only project of mass transit engaged in by the people of Fort Collins in the early years of the 20th century. In January of 1910, the great Union Pacific Railroad announced plans to build a new line and terminal facilities into Fort Collins from Denver. The citizens of the city had been hoping for a competing railroad offering quicker, cheaper and better services for freight and passengers for thirty years, so the news was met with great excitement. As in 1878, the city was very accommodating and gave the railroad everything it wanted.

The route the Union Pacific chose was along Riverside and Jefferson Street. The railroad purchased five city clocks along Jefferson Street for switching yards and a terminal building. This meant that the tracks would be laid right through the old military fort's parade ground. It also meant that the famous old Tedmon House Hotel at the corner of Jefferson and Linden would have to be torn down. The railroad also requested that the city make Jefferson Street 30 feet narrower and give the land to the railroad.

The city did everything the Union Pacific asked. It just seemed like good business to cater to the needs of the big railroad. Selling them the land from the old military fort was no problem. There was nothing left from the old fort anyway. The destruction of the historic Tedmon Hotel was also regarded as bowing to progress. The city even named the agent for the railroad, Jesse Harris, as the mayor of Fort Collins for the year in which the construction was underway and completed.

The Union Pacific kept its part of the bargain and the work got going in earnest in the middle of 1910. A work camp of 500 men was located just outside of town to house the workers laying the track. The Tedmon hotel was used as housing for the men who were building the terminal depot on Jefferson Street. When the tracks got to the terminal area, the old hotel was demolished. Altogether, the Union Pacific invested $400,000 to lay the track and build the terminal. The work was substantially finished in the summer of 1911, and on July 15th, passen-

The Jefferson Station depot for the Union Pacific railroad at its grand opening in 1911. Today it is a restaurant with the same name. It maintains the historical character of the site. Fort Collins Library

ger service began. Now the round trip to Denver could be made in less than a day and still leave time to do business in the capital city.

When The Lambkins Were King!

In the year 1910, Fort Collins had a population of 8,210 people. It had been a great first decade of the 20th century, and most people thought that it was going to go on forever. But somehow or another, the steam seemed to go out of the boom. Maybe it was the appearance of Haley's Comet in May of that year. Maybe it was the fact that Larimer County had been subdivided the year before and all of the land that was called North Park was separated to make the new Jackson County. This reduced the county to its present size of 2,800 square miles. Another 400 square miles was effectively removed from county control in 1915 with the creation of Rocky Mountain National Park.

For whatever reason, the city seemed to squat down into a period of stagnation and conservatism. A good deal of the day by day life of Fort Collins was driven by the idea of maintaining the status quo. The result was that the city didn't grow much at all for the next 40 years.

Also external forces nationally and even internationally were beginning to have a greater and greater effect on the town. No one knew it, but on the horizon were some very tough times. World War I began for the United States in 1917. Then came the world-wide influenza epidemic that killed 20 million people on earth and half a million people in the United States. Schools in Fort Collins were closed in January of 1919 because of the flu. The arrival of National Prohibition in 1920 was not such a big deal for Fort Collins since it was already a dry town.

But the roaring 20's had to be good for something in northern Colorado, so a lot of the slack was taken up by the young people. After all, just because their parents had turned up lame socially and Fort Collins had become the dullest place on earth, it didn't mean that the kids weren't going to keep things lively. Boy! Did they ever liven things up!

Everybody loves a good sports story. This one is about Fort Collins High School. It's truly a classic. In fact, if this story had come along a little bit later, it would have been an epic motion picture, a best selling novel and a television mini-series. It's about a sports dynasty that has never been seen in this country before or since. Mostly its about two men and a herd of Lambkins. It'll make you proud that you live in Fort Collins.

Beginning in 1914 and continuing clear through the end of World War II, Fort Collins, Colorado and its high school athletic teams, nicknamed the Lambkins in honor of all the lamb feeding in the Poudre Valley, were the most feared, most respected and most successful football and track and field teams in the whole United States. If you were to dig out the records of the Colorado High School football championships, you would find out that the Fort Collins Lambkins won the state championship in football more than twice as many times as all the other state champions combined. In fact, beginning in 1917 and continuing until 1936, 19 years in a row, the Lambkins took on all comers in all classes and won all the Colorado state championships.

Let me set the scene for you. It was the middle of the roaring 20's. The mostly agricultural community of Fort Collins with its population of just over 8,000 people are proud of the what they have and what they have accomplished. However, they wanted their children to have better lives and believed that education was the key to future success. Graduating from high school was a big step in that direction. Going to college was normally beyond the means of most people, so the activities and achievements of the kids in high school had many times the prominence and importance of today.

This was also the case with high school athletics, not only in Fort Collins, but all over the country. The national pastime was baseball. There was no NFL or NBA or anything even remotely resembling what we have these days. So, high school athletics had as much importance as just about anything and people really followed the schools very actively. The press gave it more coverage than today's Superbowl.

The people in Fort Collins were especially attentive since their very own Fort Collins Lambkins always seemed to have great sports teams and played anyone in the state. In those days there were no 6A or 5A and so forth. If you had an athletic team, you played whoever you wanted. The Lambkins beat them all.

These great sports teams didn't just happen. Mostly it was

all produced by a legendary coach and a never ending stream of talented over-achievers. The coach's name was George Scott. He was the coach of the football and track team. George was a good coach . . . knew all the basics . . . stuck to the fundamentals. He didn't become a legend because of that. What made him different was his keen understanding of human nature, and his ability to reach inside a kid and motivate him like none other. His players and students idolized him, hung around his house, helped him do things. He helped them all grow up.

George Scott also did something else that made a big difference. He noticed that 18 year old boys performed better than most 16 year old boys. They were also larger, taller and faster. Since there were no rules to prevent him from doing it, George would stockpile athletes. He would say to some strapping 16 year old, "You're not big enough to play football for the team yet. Go out and work on the farm for a couple of years and then come back."

And that's what they would do. By the time the kid got to high school, he was just perfect for George's football or track team. Then George proceeded to get the very best out of every player, every day.

Along about this time, in the early 1920s, one of the great deans of American sports, the famous Amos Alonzo Stagg, at the University of Chicago, organized a national high school track and field competition. It would be held annually at Soldier Field in Chicago. Any team, of any size, from anywhere in the country was invited to compete for the national championship with the best in America. Well, out here in the wilderness, George Scott, heard the call, and even though there were only about 300 kids in the whole school, he was determined to take part.

In 1924, George took his athletes to Chicago. Most of the kids had never even been out of the Poudre Valley, let alone a huge city like Chicago. So it was that they boarded a train on a spring morning in May and took off into the great world outside, to display their athletic talents at famous Soldiers Field. All the way there, George, the master psychologist, was telling his kids that all those big schools from all over the country had kids just like them. He said that they were all the same on the field and that if each one of them did his best, then he would be proud of them.

The team stepped off the train in Chicago amidst a whole lot of "oohs and aahs" among the kids and a lot of scoffing and gentle laughter on the part of the Chicago press. They thought the team was "cute." They called the boys from way out there in Fort (yuk, yuk) Collins, Colorado, population 8,000, the "Mountaineers." They just could not bring themselves to call them the Lambkins. Truthfully, it was a kind of rag tag outfit in stupid looking suits, who looked like they had just come to town on the last load of punkin's! Compared to the flashy, street-smart kids from the big cities, they were a sort of a comic relief.

Coach George Scott. He was called the "Father" of high school athletics.

All of the giggling and snickering stopped dead in its tracks when George Scott unveiled his team of talented athletes. Every time anyone turned around, little Fort Collins was nickeling and diming them to death. A second place here, fourth place there, fifth place somewhere else. The team ran, jumped, threw and vaulted their way into the hearts of the crusty old Chicago press. Fort Collins was a Cinderella team before anyone had ever used the term. The athletes sent the hard-bitten press writers scurrying for their maps to find out exactly where this Fort (no longer, yuk, yuk,) Collins, Colorado actually was. When the smoke cleared, out of the hundreds of teams from all over the country, George Scott's Lambkins had finished second.

The star of the team in 1924 was a lanky 16-year-old boy named Dan Beattie. He was just a sophomore that year, but he was big for his age and a superior athlete. He placed in three events, and it was mostly because of him that the team had done as well as it had.

Now, George Scott was not really used to finishing second

to anybody. His football teams won the state championship every year. Second was nice, even for the national track meet, but it was not enough. So George came home and went to work. He was a great strategist. It had not passed his notice that most teams in Chicago were pretty weak in the hammer throw. He reasoned that if a team could dominate in one event, that winning the National Championship would be easier. George didn't have the faintest idea of hammer throwing techniques, but he learned about it and his team worked on it. They worked on it for a whole year. By the time the 1925 National Championship rolled around again, the Lambkins had a hammer throw team to beat the world. This was in addition to the very real skills of all the athletes, led by Dan Beattie.

No shy, little, fading violets got off the train in Chicago this time. No hay seed bumpkins from way out West. The Lambkins had come to compete and then some. The Chicago sports writers no longer regarded the boys from out West as an interesting oddity. They followed their every move, especially young Dan.

The crowd at Soldier Field was certain that the team from Wenatchee, Washington was going to win the championship. They had a commanding lead with just three events to go, the discus, the pole vault and the hammer throw. Dan Beattie placed in the discus, another Lambkin won the pole vault and then came the hammer throw. The crowd watched in astonishment as the team from Fort Collins smashed every record in the hammer and swept the first three places, with Dan Beattie leading the way. The scoreboard told the story. The Lambkins were alone at the top. George Scott had what he wanted. Fort Collins was, in fact, the National Champions. This gets better, ya' know!

The winner of the National Championship was given a traveling trophy to display at their school for a year. It was a beautiful, solid silver trophy, two feet tall. Coach Scott could stand and look at it for hours, and he hated to give it up. But in order for a team to retire the trophy and keep it forever, they had to win the National Championship three times. A tall order considering that you were competing against the whole country. Still . . . hadn't George's team won the trophy once . . . against all odds? From his point of view, he was already half way there.

The Lambkins had the team to win again. It was intact from the year before and included Dan Beattie, who was now a senior. So George set out to turn these boys into fanatics. In August, before school started, George took the entire team into the mountains to work on a logging camp for a whole month. The coach watched with pride as he watched his strong, young men, throwing logs around like toothpicks and glistening with sweat in the afternoon sun. All except for one. For over there, laying under a tree and smiling at them all was Dan Beattie. Coach Scott walked over to him . . .

"Whatcha doing, Dan," asked Scott, innocently?

"Just taking it easy, Coach."

"But you're the only one who's not working."

"Aaah Coach, I'm already in better shape then all those guys."

Scott gave a knowing smile as he hunkered down next to his star athlete. "Even if that was true, which it's not, you still should be setting an example as captain of the team, and work harder than anyone else," he said.

Beattie tossed that off with a wave of his hand. "I'll set a good example when we get to Chicago."

The coach gazed seriously at the boy. "No, Dan, that'll be too late."

"What's that supposed to mean?"

"It means that winning is all done right here, right now, in everything we do. Every time you sluff off a little here, it'll cost you a little bit on the field in Chicago. If you keep going this way, the chances are you'll lose to some other kid who wanted it more."

"Ahhh, Coach."

George Scott got to his feet and took a small notebook out of his shirt pocket. "See this little black book here?" he asked.

"What about it?" answered Dan.

Dan Beattie. From the team picture of the 1925 national championship for track and field.

Fort Collins Library

The coach waved the little book in Beattie's face. "Inside this book I'm keeping track of all the times you take the easy way out, sluff off, break the training rules and don't do your best. Now I'm not going to mention this again, but I'm gonna keep on writing things down, and someday, when you are getting beat, and you don't know why, I'm gonna take out this book and read you all the times you had a chance to be better and didn't do it."

And that was all there was to it. Coach Scott didn't mention it again and Dan Beattie sort of forgot about the whole incident. He was not a bad person, just a little mischievous and frisky.

In the spring of 1926, the Fort Collins Lambkins went to Chicago for the third year. They were now the defending National Champions. The Chicago press turned out reams of copy about the "Mountaineers." They still wouldn't call them the Lambkins. They sized them up against the other great teams and wrote that the team from Columbus, Ohio would be their biggest threat.

The team from Columbus, Ohio *was* formidable. To matters worse, the Lambkins big event, the hammer throw, had now been discovered by lots of people and Fort Collins slipped to third, fourth and fifth in the event. The rest of the team was not doing so hot either. The Lambkins were falling behind the Columbus team and they were running out of time.

Now, George Scott played his trump card. He called his star over and had him sit down with him right in the middle of Soldier Field. With everything going on around them, they were effectively alone, even though there were tens of thousands of people in the stands.

With a pained expression on his face, the coach patted Beattie gently on his shoulder. "It doesn't look like we're gonna win this time, Dan," he said. "Its too bad because it didn't have to happen this way."

The boy shook his head in resignation, "We're doing the best we can."

The coach went on evenly. "You remember last August when I sat you down and told you that we weren't going to win the championship here in Chicago, but back in Fort Collins with each little thing we did to get better?"

"Sure, I remember that," said Beattie.

Scott sighed, "Do you also remember that I told you that I was keeping track of all the times when you missed a practice, broke the training rules or let yourself down . . . in this little black book right here?" He took the book out of his pocket.

Dan lowered his eyes and said simply, "Yes."

"And do you remember that I told you that someday, when it really mattered, that I was going to take out my book and read you everything I had written down?"

Beattie looked at the coach with astonishment and then said, "You don't mean . . . "

"Yes. This is the time. I can't think when it would matter more. So now you're going to listen." With that Scott opened the notebook, wet a finger with his tongue, and turned a page. "Let's see now," he began, "on August the 14th you wouldn't . . . "

And so, Coach Scott's voice droned on and on as he read one entry after another from his little book. Dan Beattie was devastated. He was overwhelmed with grief. He sobbed over his lost opportunities. Finally, Scott finished and put the book back into his pocket.

"Well," he clucked gently, "I guess there's nothing for it now. Just get out there and do your best, Dan. Who knows? Maybe it will be enough. Good Luck, Son."

A red fury smoldered in Dan Beattie's eyes. He was still the best! He was *not* going to let the team down. So Dan stormed out onto the track and grabbed a place in the 120 yard high hurdles. Then he placed third with a personal best in the shot put. Finally, he broke the American record for the discus and won the event. He had single-handedly scored half of the Lambkins total points. And it was enough. The big team from Columbus, Ohio finished second to Fort Collins, and the Lambkins became the only team to ever repeat as the National Track and Field Champion. At the awards ceremony, Dan Beattie accepted the big silver trophy that would stay in Fort Collins for one more year.

Now the last of this story goes like this. In 1927, a lot of the team, including Dan Beattie, had graduated, and the Lambkins finished second in the championship. But George Scott was not going anywhere, and he was determined to win the silver trophy for a third time and retire it to Fort Collins forever.

At the 1928 games, the team took all six places in the hammer throw and 16 Lambkins placed in other events. They easily outdistanced a team from Gary, Indiana, and George Scott had his third championship and the trophy belonged to Fort Collins and history.

Years later George Scott would be recognized in the publication "Who's Who in American Education," as the "Father of American High School Athletics." He died in Fort Collins in 1969. In 1975 he was posthumously inducted into the Colorado Sports Hall of Fame.

As for Dan Beattie, he went on to college at Colorado A and M, and then into the Fort Collins school system where he taught and worked for over 30 years. He died in 1978. Today he is remembered by the school district and the city at the school that was named for him . . . Beattie Elementary School.

The Bubble Breaks.

As the 1920s came to a close, Fort Collins and Larimer County had undergone almost forty years of unprecedented growth and prosperity. The Poudre Valley had lived up to its promise of being among the best agricultural lands on earth and for two generations the solid farmers and ranchers had brought home one bumper harvest after another. From this the city prospered and grew. Everyone agreed that they had the best of all lives here in the shadows of the great mountains.

But storm clouds were beginning to form on the horizon, both physically and economically. The people of northern Colorado could not have imagined how awful the next few years would be. It was a monstrous time and hardship and ruin were now drawing near. The agonies of the Great Depression and the Dust Storms would soon begin to blow across the Poudre Valley.

It was October 29,1929 — *Black Tuesday*. The New York Stock Exchange crashed. Nine out of every ten dollars in the stock market were obliterated. In the next four years, unemployment in the United States went from 3.2% to nearly 25%,almost a quarter of the work force. 1616 banks failed, 20,000 business firms went bankrupt and there were 21,000 suicides. Prices fell drastically in every segment of the economy, but nowhere worse than in the price of food, the same food that was being grown here.

Even before they knew what was happening to them, the people of northern Colorado were in the biggest fight of their lives. Worse, there was nothing they could do to stop it. Always before when the people of northern Colorado had tough times, they banded together and solved the problems all by themselves. But *this* was so big, so widespread, so catastrophic! The agricultural community was heavily leveraged to all the local banks. They owed for land, improvements and equipment. Plus they relied on the banks to loan money against future harvests. Now the banks had no money to lend, but still wanted to be paid on the loans from the farmers and ranchers. But the farmers and ranchers were only getting half as much money as they used to for their crops and livestock. They couldn't take care of themselves, let alone pay on their loans to the banks. So the local banks began to fail. Families who had homesteaded here in the 1860s had their property foreclosed on and they were evicted. It was devastating!

Just at the moment when it seemed as though it couldn't get worse, it did get worse. It began at almost the same time as the Depression. First, the already semi-arid lands of northern

The Dust Bowl of northern Colorado. Clouds of dust were thrown as high as 20,000 feet into the sky.   Robert L. Croissant, Colorado State University Cooperative Extension

Colorado suffered a real drought. Almost no rain fell for two years. In the days when there were only Indians and buffalo on the Great Plains, the drought resistant prairie grass protected the soil in dry times. Now most of that was gone with the land being plowed under for crops that were more suitable to the advance of civilization. The soil itself now lay naked and exposed and vulnerable. It dried and cracked under the burning sun. As the months went by and the rains did not come, the soil was pulverized and become dust as every drop of moisture was sucked out of it.

Then came a day in 1931 when all the land of the northern Colorado became deathly quiet . . . as silent as a tomb. The southern horizon began to darken and the dark spread across the sky like a black robe. In Fort Collins, the lights in the homes and buildings were lit.

Sweeping up from the south in towering clouds that reached 20,000 feet came a blanket of thick, heavy dust that grew as the winds scoured the barren lands. Wave after wave of storms blew through northern Colorado. They began with tiny balls of mud that pelted the earth, then the winds and the dust would come and last for days. When the storms blew themselves out, there would be only a few days of pleasant weather and then it would all begin again . . . month after month, year after year.

Dust was everywhere. It crept into every house, every store, every building. It went through tightly sealed windows and doors, and got into food, clothing and furniture. It clogged and choked everything. Huge drifts of fine soil piled up ten feet deep against fences. Highways were closed. There was so much electricity in the air that spark plugs in cars fired by themselves. It was difficult to tell night from day, and the lights burned in the embattled homes around the clock.

The devastation of the dust storms in northern Colorado would go on for eight years. Fort Collins was just barely hanging on. The population had grown to over 9,000, before 1930, but now thousands of people in Larimer County had moved on. People had just given up and moved away, sometimes with nothing more than the clothes on their backs. Everything was gone. It was the worst of times. It would take many years for the damage to be erased and life to return to normal. But the people of northern Colorado didn't know that and in those days of the dust storms, which reached their peak in 1935, it looked like nothing could ever restore the land and bring back the people.

Today, we know that Fort Collins did recover and emerge stronger than ever into the modern times. But those who would say that the times were not really that bad, have no conception of the monsters of the Depression and the Great Dust Storms that lay astride a prostrate and helpless Colorado.

"Rough Times And Renaissance" 1933-1953

"REBIRTH . . . *must mean that something has died. In northern Colorado, a great deal had died during the Dust Bowl years of the 1930s — crops, cattle, hopes, dreams and a sense of innocence. The Poudre Valley was not going to continue to be great, simply because it existed. The Depression and the Dust Storms had proved that. What was going to be required was nothing less than a whole new way of thinking and a tremendous amount of work. In the two decades that began in 1933, the people of the Valley proved they were equal to the task.*"

Walker speech to the
Overland Sertoma Club, 1994

Downtown Fort Collins, 1933. Trolleys roll through the intersections of College and Mountain Avenues and Linden Street.

The Grim Facts

For nearly a century, the lands of the Poudre Valley in northern Colorado had enjoyed a very favorable climate cycle. It's true that there had been floods, heavy snows and long, cold winters, followed by summers of blazing heat. But through it all, there had been enough water, to irrigate the land and grow the crops. Since the valley was a semi-arid area and averaged just over 14 inches of moisture annually, the agricultural community had adapted to those limitations by digging irrigation ditches, storing what water they could and conserving their water use.

However, there was not a lot of tolerance in these conditions. A few inches of water *less* per year, could mean the failure of an entire crop. This had occasionally happened over the years and it was always a serious blow to the economic health of Larimer County and the city of Fort Collins. Agriculture had always been the muscular engine of prosperity for all of northern Colorado.

Now it was beginning of 1933, and the Poudre Valley was suffering. Almost no rain had fallen for two years. The soil was no longer protected under a mantle of natural prairie grass. It had been cultivated for wheat and hay and a thousand other crops intended for the human population. Now the land lay bare, and exposed. Every ounce of moisture had been sucked out of the soil and it became, thick, fine, choking dust. When the wind blew, the dust flew thousands of feet into the air and blotted out the sun. Then it flew many miles and landed in ugly drifts that sifted into the irrigation ditches and piled up ten feet tall along the fence rows.

Nothing could grow very well. Small, family gardens were maintained with difficulty so that at least families would have something to eat since there was no money to buy anything. The Great Depression smoldered and festered across the nation, and Fort Collins had been immediately effected because of the sudden drop in food prices. Now, even if they had water and could grow crops, the farmers couldn't sell them for enough money to pay the costs of production. Of course, with the collapse of the agricultural and ranching community, all the other businesses in town suffered too. People were losing their jobs, their savings and going bankrupt. On every street there were empty houses of families who had just given up and moved on. There were no two ways about it, Fort Collins was in serious trouble.

Ground To Dust

At the heart of the financial and social crisis were the banks. The banks loaned money to businesses, farmers and ranchers who used the funds to operate their enterprises. When the harvest was completed, everybody paid off their loans of the previous season. Now, the farmers and ranchers could not pay any of their loans and they couldn't grow any crops. This caused the banks to go broke and everyone lost their money. However, one bank in Fort Collins refused to be "Ground to Dust!"

After Franklin Roosevelt became President in the 1932 election, the federal government declared "bank holidays," which were nothing more than attempts to stop the runs on the banks. These gave the federal bankers a chance to size up the banking industry and to close, permanently, those banks that were no longer solvent.

The bank examiners came to Fort Collins and declared that every bank in town was broke . . . except for one. This was the venerable Poudre Valley Bank that had been established in 1878 by William C. Stover. The bank examiners ruled that the Poudre Valley Bank could stay open, but only if it shed its portfolio of "bad loans." This meant that the bank was now required to foreclose on all the people whose loans had become delinquent and were unable to pay up. There were 65 of these delinquent loans. About 95% of these were agricultural loans to farmers and ranchers. With very heavy hearts, the directors of the bank prepared to foreclose on families, many of whom had been part of the Poudre Valley for generations.

The Chairman of the Board in 1933 was Benjamin Hottel. He was Fort Collins' only millionaire. He had come to the community with the railroad in 1877 and had been a prominent businessman every since. It was Hottel who had put up the lion's share of the money to build the Great Western Sugar Beet Plant in 1903. He got rich from the enterprise. In 1906, he had put up $100,000 to establish the Fort Collins Gas Company and bring gas for cooking and heating the homes of the city. He was a true builder as well as a man of compassion for the people and the circumstances of the times. He was not willing to just foreclose on all these properties and force families into bankruptcy and ruin.

So Hottel got all of the directors of the Poudre Valley Bank together in their board room at the bank that was then located at the corner of College and Mountain. This is what he told them.

B.F. Hottel. He was chairman of the board for the Poudre Valley Bank from 1910 till 1937. He and the other directors of the bank held the line against the Great Depression. The bank never closed and remained a solid financial institution under Hottel's leadership during the 1930s.   Fort Collins Library

"Gentlemen, in order for this community to survive the Depression and the dust storms, this bank must remain open. However, in order for the bank to remain open, we must dispose of all our delinquent loans. You and I both know that almost all of these loans are agricultural. They are on farms and ranches of people we have known all our lives. The federal government doesn't care about what it will mean to all these families, nor do they care how we go about it. They just are interested in the bank remaining a strong financial center for Fort Collins. Does anyone have any idea how we are going to solve this problem?"

Nobody could think of any way to comply with the bank examiners without the pain of foreclosure on all those properties. Hottel went on.

"Well, I'll tell you. I'm not willing to ruin the lives of people in that fashion. Someday, the Depression will be over, the dust storms will pass, and Fort Collins will emerge as a better town, stronger and with a future of which we can all be proud. We need all the good people we can get to rebuild all we have lost. This is what we are going to do . . . "

Hottel's solution was a model of community citizenship. He proposed that all of the directors of the Poudre Valley Bank borrow money from him and use it to purchase the properties of all the people who owed them money. He proposed that the properties be purchased from their owners at or near pre-Depression prices. This would mean that the families who owned those properties would have money to start over, hopefully right in town.

The bank directors were dumbfounded. Didn't Ben Hottel know that the chance of him recovering any of the money that was lost in these transactions were slim and none? They conservatively estimated that Hottel would get back no more than ten cents on every dollar.

Hottel was undaunted and he said, "I can afford it, and that is the way we shall have it."

So the directors of the bank borrowed money from B.F. Hottel with no interest or due dates on the loans. In turn they went out to all 65 of their customers and purchased their properties at very generous prices. The people then paid off the bank loans and used what was left for a new start. Many of them did stay in Fort Collins and stick it out through the Depression and the remaining five years of the Great Dust Storms. The directors held on to the properties and only sold one of them when they needed to pay the taxes on all the properties they owned as individuals. All the way through the

1930s, World War II and beyond, this loyal little group of bankers held the line against a world of hardship. They could have all gotten rich in what they were doing, but they didn't.

You see, there was still the matter of all these properties that the bank directors owned. We haven't exactly said which land this was. Actually it was scattered everywhere around Fort Collins. That is, Fort Collins as it looked in 1933 . . . all 2.1 squares miles of it. The agricultural land was outside of that town. This means that we are basically talking about all the land east of College Avenue to I-25, and from Prospect Street to Harmony Road. In your Dreams! Yet, that's what they had. However, in the spirit of Benjamin Hottel, the men sold the properties off steadily through about 1948. If they had held on to the land for even another five years, they would have gotten ten times to each dollar they had invested. But that's not why they were doing it. That's not what B.F. Hottel was talking about when he said the city must survive. So, in the end, most of the men settled for no more than thirty cents for every dollar they had invested.

Of course, none of this was very obvious to the people of Fort Collins in 1933, and the prospects for the city were not all that bright. Still ahead were the worst of the dust storms and a depression that seemed endless. In the final analysis, it was the little things that made the difference. It was the families, the relationships, the closeness of the community, that continued to grow this vision along the Poudre Valley.

Annie, The Railroad Dog

When the times were so bad in the early 1930s, the two or three thousand families in town had a tendency to band together and focus on living a day at a time. Traditions ran deep. No matter how hard things were, people felt they could count on each other. Life was still pretty simple. The most modern transportation that people had was the railroad. Certainly there were a fair number of cars in town by this time, but there were no interstate highways and cars were a local phenomenon. If you wanted to really get somewhere, you took the train. This meant that a lot of people went in and out of the main train station, and it was a popular meeting place.

In 1934, the train to Fort Collins steamed into Timnath on a

Annie, the railroad dog. A faithful Fort Collins institution for her entire life. Fort Collins Library

cold winter morning. Across the street from the station was a blacksmith shop and a couple of the railroad men happened to have business there. Clear at the back of the shop, the men found a little collie, barely more than a puppy. She was cold and shivering and starving. However, she must have been a real personality because she charmed those tough old railroad guys right out of their bib overalls. Times were hard in 1934, and a stray dog just didn't attract a lot of attention amidst the general misery of the age. This one did. The railroad men coaxed the little dog onto the train and brought her back to Fort Collins and gave her a home. They also gave her a name. They called her Annie. Annie lived at the Depot on Laporte Street, just off College Avenue, and she turned out to be one those rare individuals who charmed everybody.

From then on, Annie was a permanent fixture at the Fort Collins railroad depot. She was known and loved by the whole town. Whenever a trained chugged into the station, she would faithfully march out to the platform and greet every passenger. Annie was the unofficial ambassador of the city, and newcomers were often amazed to see local people get off the train and run to greet the little dog before they would their families. She never strayed very far from the station. It was her empire, and she was the reigning queen. You see, Annie had come at the worst part of the depression and the dust storms. She was a bright little light to otherwise drab and dreary days. People had come to think of her as a symbol of better times. She represented something permanent, reliable and beautiful. The citizens of Fort Collins cherished her. For the next several years, people just gritted their teeth and propelled themselves, along with Annie, into an unknown future.

The Lindenmeier Archaeological Dig.

It's an ill wind that does not blow some good. In the midst of all this catastrophe a discovery was made that was of enormous importance for the scientific community. Of course, since it did not improve peoples' lives, the discovery did not really attract a lot of attention. But taken in an historical context, the discovery was significant and effected the study of ancient man worldwide. This is the story of the Smithsonian Institutes' archaeological dig at the Lindenmeier Site, north of Fort Collins. It is also the story of the people themselves who lived so long ago and left the artifacts that chronicles their lives. If diaries had been kept in those days, then these are the words that might have been recorded as "Voices in the Wind."

"We were all happy when we crossed the last set of hills and saw the smoke from the fires in the gathering place of the people in the small valley between the two bluffs. It was a good camp, and our people had come here before the coming of each winter for as long as I can remember. It was here, three seasons ago, when I was chosen for mate by the best hunter in our clan.

Life has been good. I have a son . . . his second winter. He is strong, like his father. I think he will become a great hunter. I had another baby, a girl; but she died. All the men said it didn't matter if a girl child died, but I was sad.

My clan has a great prize to bring to this gathering. In the summer we fought and killed the great hairy beast from the northland. The one with the long, sharp tusks and the trunk that is taller than a man. I had never seen one before. My mate says that they are nearly all gone, and he has only seen a few in his life. My mate was the leader of the hunting party that killed the beast. He threw his spear into the beast's eye and the beast could not see on one side. The other men threw many spears into his side. But he fought for a very long time and killed two of our men. Now we have brought one of the tusks with us to the gathering to show that our men are mighty hunters.

This is a good camp for us. There is plenty of water, and even though the people have used it for since before even the oldest one can remember, there is still enough wood in the forest nearby so that we don't have to walk very far to find fuel for our fires. Our people use this time to hunt the herds of buffalo that travel across the land in great numbers. There are enough of us to mount a large hunting party so that many animals can be slaughtered and the meat dried for the long winter ahead when food is not so easy to find. The men tell stories of their hunts and bravery. The women gather together their children to show how much they have grown and how strong they have become. Some of the men fashion the points for our spears from the rocks that chip and flake when they are struck with the bones of antelope and deer. The younger men learn this skill from the old ones so that we have points to use during the next year.

I will see my family here if they have lived the whole year. I was picked by my mate and left my family at the gathering three years ago when I was old enough to take a mate and leave my group. Last year when we came, my mother was not with my home clan. They said that she had grown old and died during the cold winter, but my brother and sister lived still. I hope to see them this year.

I am happy to be together again. This is the happiest time of the year for us. Life is good. "

The centuries passed. The land grew warmer and it became drier. The water and the forests that were once so plentiful disappeared with the passage of time, and the ancient people no longer came to the little valley between the two bluffs. It was not used as a main gathering point anymore, and only the migrating herds of buffalo, antelope and deer crossed the land. At the beginning of the 20th century, some 100 centuries since the time of the wandering people, modern man began to take a new interest in the ancient history of North America and wonder what kind of man had once lived here and when.

In the summer of 1924, two brothers from Fort Collins by the name of Coffin came across the site 30 miles north of town while they were exploring. They were eager explorers and went out whenever they could to search for remains of Paleozoic man. The land was owned by a family named Lindenmeier, and from then on the site was known by that name.

One particular day this summer, the Coffin brothers were very excited to find a large concentration of bones, stone arrow points and other artifacts. Clearly this was not just another temporary camp used by the Indians over the years. It must have been much older than that. The Coffins dug and explored the site for a number of years in secret. They did not want the general public to know what they had found for fear that a rush of treasure seekers and amateur collectors would descend on the site and destroy it.

Over a period of years, the brothers gathered over 200 artifacts from the Lindenmeier site. One of the brothers, Major Roy Coffin, was a geologist at Colorado A and M College. He knew the site was unique, and so he selected some of the best pieces they had collected and sent them off to the Smithsonian Institute in Washington, DC.

The Smithsonian was interested, extremely interested, and in the fall of 1934, they dispatched Dr. Frank Roberts, a prominent archaeologist, to Fort Collins to see what he could find. On his first day of exploring the land and after making a few minor excavations, Roberts was not very optimistic. He told the Coffin brothers as much, but agreed to stay a few more days and continue looking. On the second day, Roberts wandered away from the main area in which the Coffins had been digging for all these years. He started to dig in a small arroyo.

The four year archaeological dig by the Smithsonian Institute at the Lindenmeier ranch site, north of Fort Collins.

Smithsonian

Almost immediately he turned up a group of ancient bones, stone points, tools and a dazzling array of artifacts. Never before had he seen such a concentration of remains in one place. Everybody was very excited. The men continued their work at this place they called, "The Big Pit" until bad weather forced them to close down for the Winter. Roberts returned to Washington with 189 specimens of perfectly formed, fluted, arrowheads chipped from flint and the bones of a buffalo of a type that had not been seen on the continent since the close of the last Ice Age, 10,000 years ago.

In the end, Roberts got his support from the Smithsonian and in the spring of 1935, he returned with a contingent of scientists. With the help of local work crews, many of who were family members of the Coffins, the dig began in earnest.

Over the next five years, the dig continued. When it was over, nearly 20,000 square feet had been excavated. 23 pits had been dug and as many as 31 men worked on the site each summer. A total of 6,000 artifacts were finally removed from the Lindenmeier site, making it the largest find of ancient man that had been discovered up until that time in North America. But more importantly, carbon dating of the artifacts showed that this man, who was to be called "Folsom Man" , had lived in the northern part of the Poudre Valley more than 10,000 years ago. That was more than twice as old as any relics or remains that had ever been found and science had to readjust its thinking and its clock on their theories of how early man actually had inhabited the North American continent. It was a large and significant discovery.

About half of the artifacts that were recovered are stored today at the Smithsonian in Washington. The remainder of the collection is still a part of the Coffin family archives or is preserved for everyone to see at the Fort Collins Museum.

The Water Imperative.

Great scientific discoveries or not, the Poudre Valley was hard pressed to manage day by day during the 1930s, but, as they say, nothing very good or nothing very bad, lasts very long. The worst of the dust storms ended in 1938, and the economy finally began to show signs of life. The farmers and ranchers rolled up their sleeves and went back to work. These

The fickle Poudre River was Larimer County's greatest asset and its greatest foe. It flowed erratically, sometimes too much, and other times not enough. It does not easily give up its water.   Fort Collins Library

Part VI: "Rough Times And Renaissance" 1933-1953   175

were tough, hard-working outfits in the first place who had been forged into solid steel by the ravages of drought and depression. Given even the most slender of possibilities, the agricultural community was not going to miss any opportunities to find a better way and a better tomorrow.

With the same spirit of their pioneer forefathers, the farmers and ranchers of Larimer County set about the job of repairing the land and restoring the soil to productive agriculture. They dredged out their irrigation ditches, cleared away the choking dust from the arterioles that criss-crossed the land. Then they poured water onto that land and brought life-giving moisture back to the soil. They planted crops and grew grass to protect the soil on fields that were not in production. They learned the lessons that nature had taught them. They learned that they must preserve their water in the good times, to allow them to survive in the bad. Most of all, they learned that they needed more water, a lot more water, to provide security, not only for their lifestyles, but for their lives themselves. It was also widely understood that the future financial security for the city of Fort Collins lay in the people realizing more of the actual potential for the area. This meant that the city had to provide the services necessary to attract companies and people with money to invest in the town. There was plenty of room to grow. That wasn't the problem. The problem was that they had to have more water in order to make this happen.

But the crimp in the hose was that there *wasn't* any more water.

Northern Colorado is a semi-arid region. The annual rainfall is just over 14 inches. The Poudre has an average annual flow of about 337,000 acre feet of water. The Big Thompson has an annual average of about 130,000 acre feet of water. That is all there is. To make matters worse, about 90% of that water comes in just three months in the spring and early summer.

The settlers arriving in the Poudre Valley in the early 1860s knew that water was going to be at a premium. Before there was a county, a territory, a state or anything else, there were water rights. In order to make the land grow crops, they had to dig irrigation canals. By the time of the dust bowl in the 1930s, the system of irrigation canals and reservoirs was very extensive in northern Colorado. But it was very obvious from the lesson learned from the droughts and the resulting dust bowls that it was not going to be enough.

The only way to get more water was to turn to the west and the mountains, which had three times the water supplies of northern Colorado and divert that water out onto the plains. It would be an engineering feat that would boggle the planners. The farmers, ranchers and the cities of northern Colorado just said, "We don't care how big of a job it is, we still have to have the water. Get it for us."

Big "T".

As the dust storms began to subside, the seven northern Colorado counties and all the major cities, including Fort Collins, Loveland and Greeley, embarked on the biggest public works project every undertaken in the state of Colorado, in cooperation with the Federal Government. It was called the Colorado, Big Thompson Water Project — "Big T."

It was a project of stupendous proportions. It would take nearly 20 years to complete and cost 163 million dollars. It was started in the middle of the Depression and the Dust Storms in 1934. An organization was formed called the Northern Colorado Water Users Association. Larimer and Weld County and the cities of Greeley, Loveland and Fort Collins all put money into the association. What they needed, however, was an authority that had the legal standing to negotiate with the Federal Government. If this project was going to be built, it would take the support of Congress to appropriate money to help build it. 163 million dollars was a tremendous amount of money in this time.

The shear size of the project was daunting. The goal was to divert enough water out of the mountains to double the water supply in the Poudre Valley. This would be about 300,000 acre feet of water, which is just as it sounds, enough water to cover 500 square miles of land with a foot of water. Well . . . that's a gigantic job!

Armed with some support from the U.S. Government, the Association formed the Northern Colorado Water Conservancy District, with legal powers to issue bonds and execute contracts. The District then submitted the plan to the people of northern Colorado for a vote. It passed overwhelmingly. The

District was given legal status, and the plan that had been on the drawing boards for 50 years was put into action.

In principal, the plan was straightforward. Go into the mountains and construct large reservoirs to collect water that would have flowed west from the Continental Divide, and then divert the water to flow east, through a series of tunnels and canals toward the high and dry plains of northern Colorado. At the end of these waterways, the plan called for several equally large reservoirs to be built to store the water. The owner of the water is the District, which means the water really belongs to the cities and counties which created the District in the first place. Upon completion of the project, the counties would then have enough water to irrigate the land and grow the crops, and the cities would have enough water to allow for ample growth and prosperity for the foreseeable future. This was the lynch pin, the anchor around which the future of Fort Collins would develop.

By 1958, all the dams, canals, feeder ditches, tunnels, hydroelectric plants and reservoirs had been built. The District continues today. In addition to operating the entire Big "T" infrastructure, the Northern Colorado Conservancy District annually sets quotas for how much of the total capacity of the system that it will release to all the users. The entire storage capacity is like a "bank" of water. It holds the excess in reserve for use in the dry years when the needs of the agricultural community and the cities must still be met. This was, of course, the whole point of the project in the first place.

Streamlining City Government.

1938 was an important year for Fort Collins and Larimer County. Not only was the Big T water project begun in that year, but other factors were combining to improve the general health of the Poudre Valley. Most of the dust storms had died out by 1938. Farm prices were improving. And because of a smart bank and a hero for a Chairman of the Board, the core of the business community was intact.

So the administration of the city of Fort Collins took a look around and decided it was time to modernize the city government. They submitted a proposal to the voters for a

Council/City Manager form of government. The outcome was quite interesting.

"No, NO, NO! NO!!!!! HELL, NO!! HUH-UH! IMPOSSIBLE! UNLIKELY! PREPOSTEROUS!"

There's just not a lot of room for doubt here, is there? Voters simply told the city "NO" in 1938 when they were asked to approve a change in the city charter that would bring a Council/City Manager form of government to Fort Collins.

Before the election, the city government had lectured the voters of the city most eloquently.

"Ladies and Gentlemen, it is time for Fort Collins to progress in a modern society and adopt the form of government that is used by almost every city of any size in the country. We have used the outdated and very inefficient "City Commissioner" form of government since 1913!

"A City Manager form of government lets us go out and hire a trained professional whose job it will be to hire a staff, run the city services including fire, police, streets, parks, and courts, all under the direction and control of an elected body of citizens who sit on the city council. It will be more efficient, cheaper and more responsive to your needs as citizens."

"NOPE! HUH-UH!, NIX! NEIN!, NYET!"

The city government got its collective plow cleaned!

How did something so reasonable and so natural to adopt, go down to such ignominious defeat? Well, the reason is because the government system of Commissioners in Fort Collins, actually worked. It worked very well indeed, and the peo-

Guy Palmes. City manager and city visionary, led the city of Fort Collins from 1938 till 1961.

ple felt more than justified about being somewhat cautious in dumping their neat old commissioners system to some high-handed professional from the outside, who they didn't know from Adam. The people just said "no thanks."

This is the way it was. Commission government worked sort of like a Presidential Cabinet. Each person, or commissioner, was responsible for some element of the government. So we had a commissioner of finance, utilities, streets, parks and so forth. The idea was to allow for the specialization of talent. A person did what he or she was good at instead of having to be all things to all people.

Well, the commissioner form of government was made just for Fort Collins. The city had a lot of people who could specialize in the various government departments. Since they never did pay the commissioners any real salaries, the people had to serve on a voluntary basis, since most of them had businesses to run or jobs to work at as well.

The weakness to the commissioner form of city government was that it was so easily corrupted. Fortunately, in the case of Fort Collins, the people who ran for commissioner were not only talented, but honest . . . as pure as the driven snow. The system worked here because it was run by the most conscientious, honest and hard working men and women that it was possible to stuff into a little town. There never was any corruption, graft, kickbacks, dishonesty, crime or any of the other horrors of the modern city.

At any rate, when the city government, meaning these very same overworked commissioners, went to the voters to change to a City Council/City Manager kind of government, the voters said no in a very loud voice. That was a setback, but not for long. The commissioners of Fort Collins knew that they couldn't keep up with all the work much longer. Besides, it was ridiculous to have the commissioner of utilities, personally go over to some lady's house and unplug her plumbing, when he had a business of his own to run. So the city commissioners did the only thing they could, under the circumstances. They hired a city manager anyway — exactly what the voters had told them they didn't want them to do.

As it turned out, there was no scandal, no special prosecutors, no outcry for recalls. There were two reasons for this. First, the idea of a city manager really was the right answer for the Fort Collins that was soon to emerge. There were only about 9,000 people in town and all of them could talk to each other in about a week. This new-fangled city manager wasn't such a bad guy after all. Things really were running better.

The second reason the commissioners got away with their little heresy, was because of the quality of the individual that the commissioners hired. His name was Guy Palmes and he was the city manager of Fort Collins from the beginning in 1938 until 1961. He was a very able administrator, highly innovative, and well-liked. In many ways, much of the character and appearance of modern Fort Collins is all because of the choices of Palmes during 23 years of administration.

The Poudre Valley Goes To War.

By 1940, the population of Larimer County had reached just over 35,000 people. This was a ten-year increase of only two thousand people over 1930. Fort Collins hadn't grown at all and was still hovering at about 9,000 citizens. But 1940 was a good year. The farmers were getting 84 cents a bushel for wheat. That was the best they had done in ten years. Things were looking up. 1941 was another good year, even though the world had grown a little unlovely, and much of it was now at war. Just as with the Great Depression, Fort Collins was drawn along in the current of events, like a chip of wood on the river, and was just as helpless.

It was a quiet Sunday morning, December 7, 1941. The people in Fort Collins had gotten up that morning and were thrilled to learn that the Fort Collins High School Lambkins had won the state championship in football, one more time. In a banner headline that spread across the front page of the Express-Courier, it said "Lambkins WIN, 7 to 6!" Christmas was in the air and the paper was full of yuletide ads. A good part of the world was at war, and the paper held a lot of news from the European Front. There was also an article by a feature writer named Jim Miller who talked about a possible invasion of Alaska.

Following breakfast and a leisurely reading of the paper, most of Fort Collins went to church. It was a warm day and so many people also went out to play golf. Many were hurrying through their Sunday dinners so they could attend a presentation of the Messiah by the Colorado A and M choir.

Just past noon, in the news room of the Express-Courier, the forerunner of the Coloradoan, the teletype wires began to chatter wildly. About the only people around at the time were a couple of reporters and an editor. The day's newspaper had been published hours before, and most people had gone home. Almost indifferently, one of the writers wandered over to the teletype. There in black, block letters the teletype was printing . . . "FLASH! STAND BY!" The reporter had never seen a "FLASH" before. It was the designation for the highest kind of news bulletin. The reporter called the others over, and they all stood there around the teletype and waited.

Soon the story began to run. The Day of Infamy had begun. The reporters stood in shocked silence as the drama occurring 4,000 miles away to the west in far off Hawaii began to unfold.

"First reports say that Japanese aircraft are bombing Pearl Harbor," the teletype said.

"What the Hell!" said one of the reporters.

The report went on. "Witnesses say that many capital ships of the U.S. Navy are burning. There are also reports that Schofield Barracks have been attacked."

"Is this for real?" asked one of the reporters.

As if to answer the question, the teletype went on, "Government sources confirm that an attack by forces of the Japanese Empire on Pearl Harbor is in progress."

There was a moment of complete silence in the newsroom among the reporters. In that moment, many choices were made. Some of them said to themselves, "This is my war to fight." Others said, "This is my war to report." All of them understood that their world would never be the same again and each of them subtly switched from a peacetime to a wartime mentality, complete with fear, doubts and the realization that the words they were reading on the teletype had become the single, largest fact in their lives. Then, as if someone had pushed a button, they all dove for a telephone.

Bad news travels fast. The news about Pearl Harbor was as bad as it could get. At the same time that the teletype in the newspaper was spitting out the story to a few astonished newsmen, millions of Americans were learning the worst for themselves on radio. Fort Collins did not have a local radio station, so people tuned to Denver stations to hear the growing enormity of the story. The concert by the Colorado A and M choir went on as planned, but the audience was very subdued, and many of them were crying.

Throughout the rest of the day and into the night, Fort Collins sat and listened to the radio. Even in the presence of obvious censorship of the reports, it was clear that the United States had received a merciless beating. The entire West Coast was wide open for an attack. In many ways, the first reaction to the bombing of Pearl Harbor was fear. A lot of people believed that the United States itself would soon hear the drone of bombers over its head. But the feeling of fear, concern and shock was very quickly replaced with a vast pool of seething resentment that whipped itself into a red-eyed rage. The sleeping giant was awake at last. Someone was going to pay for this!

The day after Pearl Harbor was a Monday. The evening newspaper reported that the United States was now at war with Japan. Actually the paper was quite low key. There was no giant headline "Pearl Harbor Bombed!" splashed across half the paper. There *was* a front page editorial that said that America must now unite together to meet the challenge of the "Jap" menace. Notice that the term "Japanese" had already been trimmed down to its wartime vernacular, overnight. In another part of the paper was a report that 27 men from Fort Collins had appeared at the local draft board for immediate induction into the armed forces. And in yet another part of the paper was a report that army corporal Steven Stuppes of Fort Collins, Colorado, had fallen in the attack in Hawaii. It would be the first of many casualty and death announcements the paper would publish in the next four years. The huge old world had suddenly grown much smaller and a lot more dangerous. If it was any consolation to the people of Fort Collins, there was an ad in the paper that said Hutchinson Drug was going ahead with its grand opening, and there was another ad for a grocery store that had a special on hamburger at two pounds for 25 cents.

Within days, following the attack on Pearl Harbor, dozens of groups, committees and organizations in Fort Collins swung into action to respond to the needs of the country. The government was very specific in its instructions to its people. If you were between the ages of 18 and 49, you were told to go and enlist in the military services. If you were staying home, which the vast majority of the people were doing, then the country needed everything — scrap iron, paper, war bond sales, rationing, conservation, calm, and attention to the task at hand. The mobilization of America's titanic industrial strength would include every man, woman, and child in the country, and that included Fort Collins, Colorado.

Very soon, young men from the Poudre Valley started to leave for the military bases. The scenes were all the same. Little clusters of friends and family would gather around a young man on the platform of the train station downtown and say their last tearful good-byes. Almost always, just as the train was about to pull out of the station, the young man would reach down and give Annie, the faithful little collie, a final pat and tell her seriously to be a good dog until he got back. Annie would bark an encouraging farewell, and then the young man was gone. Annie the railroad dog, said good-bye to them all . . . some of them for the last time.

As the years went by the Poudre Valley gave everything it had to the war effort. Within 50 miles of Fort Collins, they were growing enough sugar beets to feed the whole country, but the city was rationed for sugar along with everyone else. Larimer County grew enough beef and lamb to feed an army . . . and it did, but never kept anymore for itself than anyone else had. The oil and gas wells of the Front Range pumped enough oil to fuel every one of George Pattons' tanks, but Fort Collins citizens got along on four gallons of gas a month.

The Bombing of Timnath.

Toward the end of the war, on a spring day in 1945, World War II arrived in the Poudre Valley. Along about suppertime on March 19th, 8-year-old Jack Swets was in the corral at the farm of his folks. The farm was then, as now, right at the corner of I-25 and Harmony Road.

Suddenly there was a buzzing roar and a huge fireball erupted out in the field just a few hundred yards away. The explosion was deafening. Young Jack Swets ran into the house to tell his mother what he had seen.

Soon a small platoon made up of the sheriff, his deputies, the press and several official looking government men were pouring over the Swet's farm. They were told that an explosion had occurred in their field. Well, that was the stupidest thing the Swet's family had ever heard. Of course, there had been an explosion in their field. Why else would they call the Sheriff?

The government men explained to the family, the sheriff and the newspaper people who were standing around, that this incident was a matter of grave national security. They would not speculate any further. They swore the family to secrecy, telling them to say nothing, and they told the Express-Courier that there was not to be a word about any of this in the newspaper. They repeated that it was a matter of grave national security. Then they gathered up every tiny fragment from the explosion they could find, and left without another word, leaving all the local people standing there, shouting bad advise at each other. The sheriff was annoyed that the Feds had stomped all over his jurisdiction without so much as a "by your leave." The Express-Courier was grumbling about censorship of the press. Young Jack Swets just wanted somebody to tell him what had happened.

What actually had happened was really quite serious. It was true that an attack on Timnath by the Japanese had occurred. And it was a matter of grave national security. Between November, 1944 and April, 1945, the Japanese launched over 9,000 hydrogen-filled, paper balloons at the continental United States. Each of these balloons suspended a 26 pound, high explosive or incendiary bomb. The idea was to float these balloons across the Pacific Ocean in sufficient enough quantities to create panic among the American people, set fires and make havoc. One of the bombs actually killed six people in Oregon and started a forest fire.

Since this was the first ever example of an intercontinental weapon being used against another country, the U.S. Government took the threat very seriously. After all, they didn't know what was in those bombs. It could have just as easily been biological or chemical weapons. A total of 300 of these balloons actually made it to the United States. Three of them landed on or around Timnath, however the one at the Swet's farm was the only one that exploded. The government didn't want the Japanese to know that the balloons were getting through and causing as much trouble as they were, so that was why they hushed up the stories and kept them out of all the

Victorious GIs on troop trains like this, came home to Fort Collins. U.S. *Army*

papers. Young Jack Swets was pretty low on the "need to know" pyramid, and he didn't learn the whole story until after the war was over.

At last, in August of 1945, the war was over and the killing finally stopped. Nothing in anyone's memory could equal the effort that the country had put forth to win World War II. Fort Collins had sacrificed and played its part along with everyone else. 256 boys from the Poudre Valley had paid with their lives. On VJ day the Express-Courier ran the story of Japan's surrender, and right next to it was finally the whole story of the bombing of Timnath that had been kept under wraps until that day.

The boys who had gone away to war, now began returning to Fort Collins, older, wiser, and eager to get on with their lives. Everyday, they could be seen staring anxiously through the windows of the train as it chugged into the station in Fort Collins.

Once again the scenes of families, friends and loved-ones gathering around the soldiers and sailors were repeated, but with a much happier outcome. And in the midst of all this, the faithful railroad collie, Annie, was there to bark a greeting and welcome home each favorite son. It was not at all uncommon to see, tough, veteran, battle-weary men sink down on the station platform and take the little dog in their arms and cry for joy, while Annie licked their faces and dried their tears. In those moments, each man knew that he was really home, and the war was truly over.

Post-War Poudre Valley

At the end of 1945, the United States found itself the big winner of World War II. It was the strongest country on earth. It was big, brash, swaggering and 140 million strong. The years of the Great Depression were now only memories. America retooled its wartime industrial capacity for domestic and consumer goods, which were gobbled up by the entire country who now had money and were interested in a *much* better life than what they had just spent a generation going through. It was much the same in Fort Collins.

In 1946, Fort Collins was busy shaking off the ravages of all the lousy things they had been putting up with for so many years — dust storms, depressions, drought, war, rationing and hoping somebody in your family didn't get killed. Enough!! The population of the city began to grow again and by the end of the year, reached nearly 10,000.

People were paying 25 cents a gallon for gasoline, a nickel for a coke, 8 cents for a dozen eggs, 15 cents for a loaf of bread, hamburger was a quarter a pound, a quart of milk was 21 cents, a man's new suit was $50, and a new house cost about $4,000.

There was now money to buy all of these things. Just as they had done in the past, when the good times returned, the people of Fort Collins starting thinking about improving, growing and prospering.

Foremost on the agenda was the completion of the Colorado, Big Thompson Water Project, "Big T." It had been somewhat interrupted by the war. Soon the mammoth project was in full swing.

The first thing they did was to build Granby Reservoir and Shadow Mountain Reservoir. These two huge water storage

The gigantic Big "T" water project required gigantic machinery. This, custom-made, paving machine is completing a section of one of the feeder canals.

Northern Colorado Water Conservancy District

lakes, gathered water that would have naturally flowed west across the Continental Divide and diverted it to the Front Range through the 13.1 mile long Alva Adam's tunnel. This tunnel was dug by hand and very primitive machinery! It was an incredible feat, the tunnel was wide enough to drive a jeep through it. Finally, all this water would flow into two equally huge reservoirs that would be the largest bodies of water in Larimer County, to be called Carter Lake and Horsetooth Reservoir.

Construction on Horsetooth Reservoir began in 1946, right after the end of World War II. The site selected was one of the most historic parts of the whole Poudre Valley. At the south end of where the reservoir would fill, was the little town of Stout. It had been the principal quarry for all the high quality red and brown sandstone of which so many of the buildings in Old Fort Collins had been built. Throughout the valley, running north, there were farms and ranches and homesteads, and roads running out of each of the three canyons that faced the plains to the east. At the far north end, the valley would be sealed off with a large dam, just above Bellvue, Pleasant Valley and Laporte. There was considerable heartaches over losing land in the Horsetooth Valley by the people who lived there. There was something very permanent about having the place you used to live being covered up with 200 feet of water.

Still, the job was done and most people gave in to the inevitable gracefully, in favor of realizing the dream of water that had filled the settlers heads for so many years. By June of 1947, the Adams tunnel was completed. Construction on the reservoir continued. The three canyons facing east were filled with dams and the largest dam was built on the north end.

The people of Fort Collins thought all of this was just great. All during the years of construction of Horsetooth Reservoir, people would drive along the construction roads and marvel at the work. Huge amounts of rock were stripped off the surface of the foothills that faced Fort Collins to make the big dams.

They were huge, ugly scars that looked awful for years. Probably today, they wouldn't let them do that, but the city was so much smaller then, and it needed the water so much.

Construction on the dams continued through 1947 and 1948. The town was suddenly alive with new construction of its own. For the

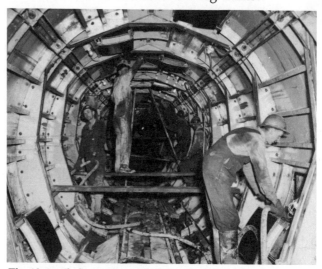

The 13.1-mile-long, Alva Adams tunnel. Dug, largely by hand, during the 1940s, it carries water from Granby Reservoir to Horsetooth Reservoir and Carter Lake.

Northern Colorado Water Conservancy District

first time, residential areas were being built south of Prospect Street and west of Shields. There was a great sense that the future potential for Fort Collins was nothing less than spectacular. But there was one soul in town whose work was now finished, and whose life was near its end.

"She Was Our Soul".

The railroad engine chugged into the station on Mason Street, just off Laporte Avenue. It was a short train. Not very many passengers rode the train these days. Most people now were finding it more convenient to use their cars since the roads had been enlarged and improved. They had even started to build a thing called a Freeway in Denver.

Nevertheless, the arrival of the train was the signal for Annie, the railroad station collie, to struggle to her feet and valiantly meet every passenger with a little woof and a wag of her tail. Her arthritis had gotten so much worse in the last couple of years, that it was getting harder and harder for her to get around.

At last, the tough, old railroaders just could not let her suffer any more. In her 14th year, she was put to sleep. Fort Collins wept. Annie had seen them all through the tough times. There had been times in the past when the only thing that seemed right about the city, was that little dog. The men of the Colorado and Southern railroad broke all the rules and buried Annie right next to the tracks where she had spent her life. And they also put up a three foot tall headstone that said, "From C and S Men, to Annie . . . Our Dog." The gravesite was destroyed some years later when the tracks were repositioned, but the gravestone is preserved today at the Fort Collins Museum.

As if all of this was a part of some grand plan, disaster struck the Poudre Valley just six months later. In January, 1949, the worst blizzard in the history of Larimer County blew through in a ferocious frenzy. Thousands of cattle froze to death as they became buried in snow. This was despite the efforts of the Air Force who dropped thousands of tons of hay in "Operation Hay Life." The road between Fort Collins and Wellington was snowed shut, stranding dozens of cars. Three people died in their cars, frozen to death. Four ranch families east of Wellington were caught in the storm and froze to death right in their homes. It was a terrible disaster.

Dawn Of The Modern Age.

Fort Collins and Larimer County was on a roll! Nothing was going to keep them from getting on with this new age that everyone was always seeing and hearing about. Construction resumed on the dams of Horsetooth Reservoir. By the end of 1949, the huge reservoir was finished and ready for water.

For the next two years, the reservoir was empty, but in late 1951, water began to flow in. It took several years to fill it up, but when it was done, Horsetooth was seven miles long and held 156,000 acre feet of water. Carter Lake was begun in 1950 and completed in 1952. Big T was now in nearly full operation and the grand plan of delivering enough water to meet the needs of a thirsty Poudre Valley was realized.

The moment had come. With the completion of Horsetooth Reservoir and Carter Lake, it was now possible to plan and dream on a scale that would have seemed unthinkable to the people of Fort Collins in the previous century. Now the Poudre Valley and all of northern Colorado had WATER . . . LOTS OF WATER!! With a resounding splash, a new cycle of growth was about to commence.

Stepping onto center stage were the characters and institutions that would propel Fort Collins into the modern era. Fort Collins was an "Undiscovered Gem." All they had to do was get the word out. They had just the man to do the job.

In 1938, when the voters of Fort Collins had rejected the idea of changing the city government from a Commissioner Form to the City Council/City Manager type, the city commissioners had defied the voters and hired a city manager anyway. This was the venerable Guy Palmes. He had been acting as the city manager for all these years, and with the completion of the reservoir, he was darn well going to figure out a way to

Inside Horsetooth Reservoir in 1951. The reservoir is finished, but still empty. Notice the two dams. On the left is Horsetooth Dam on the north end of the reservoir.

Northern Colorado Water Conservancy District

get the town growing. By 1952, the new boom was underway. Fort Collins was about to begin the longest period of sustained growth and prosperity in its history.

In that year, Fort Collins had a population of about 12,000 people. The city itself was about 3 square miles. There were four traffic lights in town, all on College Avenue. Prospect Street was a dirt road in both directions from College Avenue. It was also the city limits. From that point south, College Avenue narrowed to two lanes and became Highway 287 to Loveland, a full 13 miles away. There was one high school, one junior high and a growing number of grade schools to handle the children of the baby boom whose families were pouring into town. The phones had no dials. If you wanted to talk to somebody, you asked the operator to connect you.

But the city was stirring in a way in which it had never done before. The college, Colorado A and M, was bursting at the seams from all the students who had come to get a degree on the G.I. bill. New businesses and enterprises were coming

Horsetooth Reservoir in 1963. It is seven miles long, 200 hundred feet deep and holds 156,000 acre feet of water. Northern Colorado Water Conservancy District

Visions Along The Poudre Valley

to town, providing large numbers of jobs and stimulating growth in every other section of the economy.

It was an exciting, vibrant time! It was a time of which the earliest pioneers had dreamed, but never really believed would arrive. It was everything they could have hoped for and so much more. It was a new city, poised on the edge of greatness. As 1953 broke on the horizon, a population of new emigrants and families steeped in generations of tradition woke to a bright morning and a glorious vision along the Poudre Valley.

Part VII

"So Dear To
My Heart"
1953-1995

"FORT COLLINS . . . is more than just a town. It's a
state of mind. How we handle defeat is at least as
important as how we handle victory. One of the
most amazing things about the people who have made
up this community is that they always have felt special.
For that reason, they have never believed that any challenge was too great or that they couldn't figure out the
right thing to do when the time came. That is a rare
commodity in this day and age. It is a strength we are
going to need, a lot, in the next 100 years."

Phil Walker,
Radio Broadcast Editorial, 1995

A slumbering Fort Collins at the dawn of the modern age. This 1950 view shows the 3.1 square miles that was the home of 12,000 people.   Fort Collins Library

Before The Dawn

By the early 1950s, Fort Collins had put almost all the pieces together to produce a new boom cycle for the city. At the top of the list was the completion of Horsetooth Reservoir, which supplied all the water the city would need for the next 50 years, no matter how fast it grew. The city administration was actively encouraging development of all kinds — commercial and residential — and was working hard to keep up with the demand. Finally, the college was coming to life. Colorado A and M was expanding to meet the expected explosion of students that promised to send enrollment through the roof.

But the beginning of this story starts just before the dawn of this remarkable period of transformation. It occurs at the moment in which Fort Collins was still quiet and undisturbed, and we view it through the eyes of an eight-year-old boy.

"It was early in the summer of 1951. The air was clear and clean. Pure white, fluffy clouds floated by in a sea of deep, electric blue. The trees, bushes, and grass were all green and lush. All along the wide streets of town were neat houses with colorful flowers blooming in all directions. It was warm and pretty, and it was great to be alive. Best of all, we were MOVING!

"We had been living by city park, close to the lake. Now we were moving all the way across town, way over on the other side just three blocks from the high school. Our new house, on which my dad had done most of the building, was on Petersen Place, a half block off Prospect Street to the south. It was almost in the country, and it was a full THREE miles from our old place. About as far as you could go and still stay in the city limits of a town. My world was bounded by city park on the west, Whedbee Street on the east, downtown in the north and Prospect Street on the south.

Now moving day had finally arrived, and I had magnanimously volunteered to do my part by "moving" my bicycle, with me on it, across town. I had shrewdly reasoned that this was also a way of getting out of all that hard, boring work for a while. Well, my dad indulged me, and now I was pedaling across the whole town, all by myself. It was a beautiful day. No wonder I was in high spirits.

"I rode down Mulberry to Shields. I ignored the stop sign as I crossed the street. There was no traffic in sight anyhow. A few blocks ahead, on the left, was Lincoln Junior High School. Today it is the Lincoln Center. Then it was a three-story brick building and the only junior high in town. I went south on Howes and entered the Colorado A & M campus through the Oval. The entire university was wrapped around the Oval. There was plenty of space for the 3,000 students.

"As I worked my way toward College Avenue, I encountered the only place in my voyage that made me nervous, which was crossing that busy street. There was no traffic light at Pitkin, where I wanted to cross. As a matter of fact, there were only three traffic lights in the whole town. They were on College Avenue at the intersections of Laporte, Mountain and Olive. Out here near the edge of town there was none of that, and you had to be more cautious. My father had reminded me to be careful, but he didn't seem to think that it was beyond the abilities of an eight year old.

"I looked both ways up and down College Avenue. The traffic was unusually heavy that day. There must have been half a dozen cars within sight. None of them were very close, so I scampered quickly to the center median just in time to wave to the conductor and the people riding on the trolley as it rolled by on the way downtown in the center of the great street.

"I cut through the campus of the high school to save some pedaling. Someday I was going to go to that school, and I couldn't wait. Then I zigzagged over to Petersen Street, crossed Prospect which was a dirt road, and onto Petersen Place, also a dirt street, to my new home, second one on the left. Our house was on a big lot. It had a large hole dug in the back for the unheard of idea of building a swimming pool there someday.

"So that's the way it was in the summer of 1951. It was a quiet town, even sleepy. There were, perhaps, 3000 families living in Fort Collins, maybe a total of 12,000 people. It was the kind of a town in which an eight year old could ride his bike across in 30 minutes and be perfectly safe to do so. We never locked our houses. We left the keys in our cars and when we drove, we never signaled our turns because everyone knew where we were going anyway."

The Pieces Come Together.

But powerful forces were at work. For better or worse the curtain was about to go up on one of the most remarkable stories of growth, expansion and prosperity in the entire United States. Fort Collins was about to be discovered.

Several factors contributed to the emergence of Fort Collins as a little town to a thriving metropolis, not the least of which was that the lifestyle to be enjoyed here was simply superior to about 99% of the rest of the world. But also there was the completion of the Big Thompson Water project and its principal receptacle reservoir, Horsetooth with its 156,000 acre feet of water. Now there was enough for both agriculture and much a larger urban population.

The next thing that made the town grow was the aggressive and supportive role of the city government. The man who had been city manager since 1938, and was presiding over all this change was Guy Palmes. He was sitting in his office one day, looking out the window and wondering what he could do to give the city a shot in the arm and start people building homes and starting businesses. He worked and worked and studied and found out that the latest rage among cities in the United States was to beautify their towns by undergrounding all the utilities and getting rid of all the unsightly power lines on poles that were cluttering the landscape. Palmes learned that the cost for doing this was very expensive. It would be cheaper though in the long haul, because the power lines lasted longer underground, but the up front cost was enormous. Most cities were charging between $500 and a $1000 per residential lot to do the work. Palmes got together with the City Light and Power director, and the two of them hatched a plan to underground all Fort Collins utilities and charge only $50 per lot for new construction. Well, in an age when a whole house cost about $5,000, including the lot, this represented a huge savings.

Developers and home builders now had an excellent incentive to build more houses and attract more people and business to town. And they did. It wasn't very long before the outside world began to notice. People would come to town, drive up and down the nice, wide streets with the neat rows of houses and say, "Gee, this is really nice . . . Let's move here." All this time, crafty old Guy Palmes knew that they were moving to town as much for what they didn't see as for what they did.

The city administration thought the time was right to go back to the voters and see if they couldn't get them to approve the change in city government they had turned down in 1938. The city commissioners still believed that Fort Collins would be better served by a City Manager/City Council form of government. Guy Palmes had been hired as city manager back in 1938 in open defiance of the voters wishes, but it had turned out to be a good thing since Palmes was such a good administrator.

The city went about it in the right way. They went out and lobbied for the support of the League of Women Voters, the Chamber of Commerce, and the principal service clubs in town. When the vote came in 1954, the voters overwhelmingly approved the changes in the city charter and Fort Collins officially became a City Manager/City Council form of government with five council persons. There have been both men and women in the council right from the beginning.

The Baby Boom that got started after World War II was getting ready to go to school. This meant that in just a few more years that all those kids would be wanting to go to college. So Colorado A and M college started planning for the future with an extensive plan of expansion. Enrollment at the school was less than 3,000 students in the early 1950s. There was nothing there except for the buildings around the Oval and a block or so toward College Avenue. It was a small school. But that was going to change in a big way. In May, 1957 Colorado A and M officially became Colorado State University. Construction began on new residence dormitories to the west of the Oval. They built enough of these dorms to house at least another 5,000 students, effectively doubling the student enrollment. Now CSU was the largest employer in town, by far. It brought all sorts of new money, new people and new growth to Fort Collins.

Fort Collins was now two worlds. The big dynamics of plentiful water, aggressive city management and an evolving university had lit the fuse of growth and new people were pouring into the city. But day by day it was not so noticeable to most people. The town and, particularly, its school age children were still living their lives in the traditional ways that had been a part of our culture for generations.

All The Best Teachers In One Place.

Of course, all of this growth was completely lost on yours truly. About the only thing I worried about was how I could beat Dick Boggs home from Harris School on my bicycle during the lunch break. The Bogg's lived next door to us on Peterson Place. They had five kids and a business stuffed into a two bedroom house with a basement. They made "Bogg's Chocolates." It was the best candy I ever ate in my life. By that time I was ten or eleven and I thought I had died and gone to heaven. I lived next door to a candy factory! It was here that I learned a very valuable lesson.

The first time that I was invited to come into the inner sanctum where they actually wrapped the candy and put it into boxes, I was told to sit down and help wrap the candy. Mr. Boggs told me seriously, "We can't have any candy going out that is cracked or messed up."

"What do I do with the 'bad' candy," I asked?

"Oh, you can eat any of that," he said. "In fact, eat all the candy you want."

Guess what? I ate all the candy I wanted, and then some. It made me sick. For years after that I never more than nibbled on any of their candy, even though I must have wrapped 100,000 pieces. The moral being that you just can't drink the whole ocean even though someone is holding it to your lips. I'll bet Mr. Boggs knew that.

Dick Boggs and I were in the same grade, and in 1955 we were taking the bus or riding our bikes in good weather to Lincoln Junior High. Even in those early days the schools were already getting crowded because of all the growth, especially in the lower grades, and so we were sent off to junior high in the sixth grade. It was the big time! In the seventh and eighth grades we got to move from room to room for our classes with different teachers for every subject.

Now this is not the same Lincoln Junior High as today. The school was located where the Lincoln Center is. In fact part of the school building was saved from the wreckers ball and used to build the new Lincoln Center. Even today, I can't go to a dinner or a social function in the big ballroom without remembering that this used to be the gym where I wrestled and played volleyball with a hundred other sweaty 12 year olds.

You know you are getting old when they start naming all the new schools in town after teachers you had. Well, Lincoln Junior High had a lot of them. These days, they are just names on buildings; but to me they were and are living people. Shepardson, Linton, Lopez, Johnson, Olander, Bauder, Warner, Kruse and more. They were all there in the same school at the same time. They were good enough to have schools named after them, and they were good enough to make sure I got a fine education.

Margaret Shepardson. One of the finest teachers in the history of the Fort Collins school system. Shepardson Elementary School is named for her.　　Fort Collins Library

I took my first course in Colorado History in the eighth grade. The teacher was Wayne Linton (Linton Elementary.) Now I suppose that I read somewhere that Stephen Long led an expedition to Colorado in 1820 and wrote on his map that all of this we live in was actually, "The Great American

Desert." That's not how I learned it. What happened was that Mr. Linton held up a picture of a lush landscape with trees and fields of corn and lakes and said, "Does this look like a desert?"

"Of course not," we all said in unison!

Mr. Linton smiled and said, "Why do you suppose Stephen Long was wrong?"

So he started to tell us stories about how all of this came to be. One story led to another and another and before I knew it, the semester was over. Even though I learned a lot, the more important lesson was that history could be fun when you put a little flesh on the bare facts and dates. Works pretty well, doesn't it? No wonder they named a school after him.

For telling stories AND setting a good example, the unquestioned champion was Margaret Shepardson. She was my English teacher in both seventh and eighth grades, 1956 and 57. She was elegant, sophisticated and quite articulate, with a wonderful vocabulary. She never raised her voice, never shouted and never seemed to be in a hurry. She was patient, understanding and loving. She used sign language. When she put her finger to her lips, just so, and looked at me knowingly, it meant, "I think you are chewing gum, young man, but I'm too polite to mention it. Please dispose of this gum in as quiet and unobtrusive manner as possible and we won't mention it again." Now that's articulate! One little gesture. When she talked, she was even better.

The most memorable of all the stories she told was of her trip to Germany to see the Passion Play at Oberammergau. There were no video cameras in those days, hardly any audio-visual aids at all. So she told the story of her trip with postcards that she had collected and she tacked them all in a row around the room. She would walk from card to card and tell the story of this experience. It wasn't just all about the story of the Passion Play, it was history of it: how the whole town participated; what the German people were like; and what the countryside was like. It took her two weeks. Without a doubt, the most spellbinding story I had ever heard in my life. Even today, the memory is still fresh and in living color.

Sometime later, when I had been working at KCOL radio for several years and was trying as hard as I knew how to sound as articulate and as knowledgeable as Miss Shepardson was, she actually called me one day when I was on the air.

The telephone rang and I answered it, "KCOL Radio."

"Phil Walker?" the voice on the other end asked. "Yes it is," I said in my most pleasing and mellifluous tone.

"This is Margaret Shepardson calling," she said. "I had to, you know, because you just made a mistake in grammar in that last announcement you read."

I sat there like an idiot, not knowing exactly what to say. Finally, I blurted out, "I didn't know you listened to me on the radio!"

"Oh yes, I often do," she said in that absolutely perfect English, "It helps me keep up with my former students. But don't try to change the subject, young man. We were talking about grammar."

"Yes, Ma'am."

"In your previous announcement you said that someone should use two teaspoonfuls of something in a recipe."

"Yes, Ma'am."

"Now Philip, you should remember from our class that it is not two teaspoonFULLS. It is two teaSPOONSfull."

"Yes, Ma'am."

"You do remember the rule now, don't you?"

"Yes, Ma'am." then she stuck in the knife.

"I often have to 'tsk, tsk', at the silly language you use . . . and in public, too. Nevertheless, this most recent example of fractured English was particularly egregious, and I just had to call. Well, good-bye, Philip. Keep up the good work."

Egregious . . . ! That is the exact word she used. Go look it up yourself. I had to. When I was in the seventh grade she would have said "glaring" or "outrageous." Now I was older, and she felt that I should progress to more complex language. Today, I always have to smile when I drive by Shepardson Elementary School in Nelson Farm since they remind of the lady herself, and a neater, sweeter time.

Too Much, Too Soon.

The cycle of expansion was in full stride. It now looked like the population of the city was going to more than double in ten years. More than doubling a population of any town in ten years will cause all sorts of growing pains, and it was no different here. Everyone was going all out to meet the mandates of strong growth. In the process some very important and long-lasting decisions were made.

The traditional end of the city limits had always been Prospect Street. It was here that all of the originally platted streets from Franklin Avery's time in 1873 came to an end. Those are the streets that are so wide, at a hundred feet. Toward the end of the 1950s, the developers came to the city and proposed that new subdivisions be designed in the modern fashion for that time and built south of Prospect and west of Shields. The thinking called for curved streets, cul-de-sacs, lots backed up to each other with no alleys, underground utilities, *and* smaller lots with narrower streets. It was called "cluster design" with homes arranged around little parks, greenbelts and other amenities. Well the city thought it was a great idea. Everyone thought it was a great idea and that this must be the subdivisions of the future. So that's what they built.

The first big example of the modern subdivision was South College Heights which lay south of Prospect and along College Avenue for half a mile to Drake and east all the way to Stover. But the problem that nobody seemed to think about was that there were no big thoroughfares or even feeder streets through the subdivision. What this meant was that large through streets like Petersen and Whedbee, were cut off at Prospect. Had these wide streets been continued all the way to Drake, it would have eventually taken much of the pressure off College Avenue.

So hemmed in by South College Heights on the east and the railroad and the University on the west, College Avenue became the single big pathway to the south, where all of the growth was heading. That committed the street to become a largely commercial road and, in just a few years, people were complaining about the ugly strip city that we were building.

You see, Fort Collins was now changing, rapidly. By 1960 there were 25,000 people in town, with more arriving every day and no slowdown in sight. To a lot of people, the growth was a runaway train that brought the prosperity and economic good fortune, but also brought problems and unrest. With all of the previous expansions of the city, there had always been a period that followed in which the people had a chance to pause and catch their breath. But this time, the growth didn't stop. The people of Fort Collins, natives and newcomers alike, were just going to have to do the best they could, and the strain was starting to show.

After a decade of unparalleled growth and prosperity of the kind that make your head spin, the wheels started to fall off in 1961. This was the year in which Guy Palmes, the wily city manager for the previous 23 years, retired. During the next ten years Fort Collins had three city managers. None of them lasted very long. In all fairness to a couple of these men, Fort Collins didn't know itself what it wanted in those days. Everything was in a state of upheaval.

The explosion of growth was grinding everyone to a pulp. To make matters worse, everybody had an idea on what ought to be done to manage all this growth in an orderly manner. However, the days of being able to sit down and thrash out the problems in a city council meeting, with a significant portion of the population participating in a spirited debate, as they had been doing for the past 100 years, was over. Now there were just too many people. The public systems were just too big, the needs of the community were too pressing, for the overburdened city council to handle on their own. The debate droned on for years, and it began to look like it would never be settled.

The Great Downtown Fire.

In the middle of this tumultuous dialogue, one of the signal events of our history occurred. As with most of the big stories, this one was tragic and destructive and came unexpectedly without warning.

During most of the 1960s, Fort Collins' main business activity was still confined to downtown. The place where the Foothills Mall was built was still a farm owned by a family named Snyder. The chain stores . . . Sears, Penney's and the principal local businesses all were headquartered within a block or two of the intersection of College and Mountain. The largest department store in town was called the State Dry Goods, and it was owned locally by the Johnson family. It was a grand two story brick building at the corner of College and Oak, where the Oak Street Plaza is today. Oak Street was still open to traffic across College Avenue and the old Post Office was still in

State Dry Goods building at the corner of College and Oak in the days before the fire. It was a leading business for Fort Collins.

operation. The State Dry Goods building was across Oak street from the post office facing College Avenue.

Just after 9 p.m. on June 28, 1965, a short circuit occurred in an electrical box in one of the display windows facing College. Sparks from the short circuit rained down on the highly flammable clothes in the display window and a small fire began to burn.

The fire burned inside the State Dry goods building, uncontrolled and undetected for over an hour, until all of the oxygen in the building had been consumed. This caused the flames to go out, but the fire itself was a glowing, super-heated mass that was smoldering at several hundred degrees, waiting for a breath of fresh air to give it life once again.

At 10:30 p.m., one of the huge, quarter-inch plate glass windows shattered, blowing glass clear across College Avenue. The fresh air rushed in and a huge backdraft caused the fire to violently reignite. The entire State Dry Goods building exploded in a jarring concussion that woke up half the town.

Within minutes every piece of fire equipment in the whole city was racing toward downtown Fort Collins. Firemen arrived to find the building and the entire corner of College and Oak,

Part VII: "So Dear To My Heart" 1953-1995

fully involved in flames that were shooting hundreds of feet into the air.

Also arriving, and setting up a mobile broadcast transmitter just west of the old Post Office on Oak Street, was a 21-year-old radio announcer who was caught with a live microphone for the next two hours . . .

"Once again, from downtown Fort Collins, this is Phil Walker with more of our continuing coverage of a major fire which has destroyed most of the State Dry Goods building at the corner of College and Oak.

For those of you who may be just joining us, let me bring you up to date on the events that have happened here tonight.

An all-alarm call for all available fire fighting units in Fort Collins, with support coming from as far away as Loveland and Wellington, was made at approximately 10:30 tonight when the State Dry Goods building suddenly erupted in a fireball of flame. Eyewitnesses say that the entire building seemed to explode like a bomb and that flames shot into the sky at least two hundred feet. By the time that fire units arrived the building was completely engulfed in flames. The building houses, not only the State Dry Goods, but also a drug store and Bowen's Book Store. There are no people believed to have been inside any of the businesses when the fire broke out.

The fire has now been burning, out of control, for over an hour and a half. Police have cordoned off the entire downtown area from literally thousands of curious spectators who are lining the police barriers in hopes of seeing the fire.

The greatest danger, according to Fire Chief Cliff Carpenter, is that the fire will spread to the other buildings along the west side of the 100 block of South College. Most of the these buildings were built before the turn of the century, and the firewalls between them may not be enough to keep the fire from spreading.

The new snorkel truck with its 85-foot hydraulic boom is currently positioned above the fire on the north side of the building and is concentrating all of its water right on the firewall as a deterrent to the fire spreading down the street.

The cause of the fire is not known at this time.

The fire has now burned through both the basement and

The terrifying second in which the south wall of the State Dry Goods building collapsed in an avalanche of bricks and fire. The dark figure under the wall, as it fell, was Fire Chief Cliff Carpenter who was killed.   Fort Collins Library

Part VII: "So Dear To My Heart" 1953-1995   207

the second floor and a few minutes ago, just after midnight, the entire roof collapsed into the interior of the structure. All that remains of the building is the front along College Avenue and the exposed south side along Oak street from the alley to College Avenue.

We are located just across the street on Oak, west of the Post Office. The south side of the State Dry goods building is a brick wall, about thirty feet high topped with heavy concrete masonry that sticks out a couple of feet. There are several windows on this wall and fire is shooting out of them. The heat, even from here, about a hundred feet away is intense.

Currently firemen are working along the wall and have several hoses running through the open windows in hopes of getting to the main fire deeper inside the building. Fire Chief Cliff Carpenter is directing this work. In fact, a little while ago I saw him give one of his exhausted men a break on one of the hoses and man it himself. The fire is . . .

My God, the entire wall has just collapsed! I saw two or three firemen running away from the falling bricks to just barely escape being crushed under all those tons of materials! But I think there were at least two men who were caught by the falling wall! Dozens of firemen, police and even bystanders are now furiously digging in the rubble to try and uncover the men! We have no word on just who could be under that rubble or their condition, but Chief Carpenter was manning a hose just under the wall when it collapsed and I don't see him now! Ambulances are moving into position!

The firemen are now removing the last of the bricks so they can get whoever is trapped under there out! I can see one man who has been uncovered by the firemen, and he is now being placed on a stretcher! There is a tremendous amount of excitement near where the first fireman was recovered! They are now taking a second man out of the rubble! I can't see . . . Oh my God! It's the Chief! Boy! I hope he's OK!"

The Chief was not OK. He was pronounced dead on arrival at the Poudre Valley Hospital. Fire Chief Cliff Carpenter is the only Fort Collins fireman who has ever died in the line of duty in our history. The second fireman was seriously injured, but recovered.

The 60s Turn Out To Be A Bummer.

The 1960s were a tough decade for Fort Collins. As the years rolled by, the city continued to grow explosively. By 1970, the population was 50,000 people. It had now grown four times larger than at the beginning of the expansion in 1950. The city administration was falling behind in providing facilities for recreation, public information and the arts. The city administration was hard-pressed just to keep up with all the new streets, curbs, gutters, water, gas, electricity, and sewers in the crazy-quilt pattern of new subdivisions that were sprouting up endlessly.

Many voices were now being raised regarding the imperative of maintaining Fort Collins unique quality of life. It is a debate that has never had an end and goes on even into the present day.

People who had moved to Fort Collins because it was a wonderful town to raise kids and run a business, were now complaining that all this uncontrolled growth was wrecking the quality of life they had moved here to enjoy in the first place. They viewed the natives as being greedy, self-indulgent and too proprietary about the town.

Fort Collins long-time residents had some complaints of their own about all the newcomers. They said that they were taking the attitude that now that they were here, that we should slam the door and not let anybody else in. They also did not like the idea of all these new people coming to town and telling the natives what to do and how to do it.

Both groups would have been interested to know that almost exactly the same kind of debates had occurred in 1873, 1880 and 1910. These dates corresponding approximately to the three previous periods of fast growth in the history of the city. In each of those periods, the natives were highly annoyed that all of the newcomers were moving to town and telling them how the city should be run.

It was also a lousy decade for the country. The United States had to endure the Cuban Missile Crisis and a close brush with a real nuclear war, the assassinations of President Kennedy, his brother and Martin Luther King. But no issue more thoroughly polarized the American people quite as much as the Vietnam War.

Fort Collins was exposed to all of this upheaval in a kind of detached sort of way. The people of town were certainly aware of the many debates going on all over the country on the Vietnam War. But that was just the beginning. They also were listening to debates on the environment, education, free speech, drugs, the military-industrial complex, nuclear missiles, civil rights, gender gaps and poverty. It was endless.

How do you suppose the good people of Fort Collins handled all this rhetoric? They tuned it out. They ignored as much of it as they possibly could, partly as a defense mechanism to keep from getting overwhelmed, but mostly because not much of it seemed to be vitally pertinent to their lives in this city. There were no military bases here, no napalm factories, no significantly militant minorities, no large concentrations of hard-core hippies, no huge crime waves, no drug epidemics — none of that stuff. And the people of Fort Collins were very glad to be left out of the national debates. Fort Collins was blessed. Its quality of life was undisturbed. Money magazine listed Fort Collins as one of the ten best cities in the country in which to live and raise a family. It looked like the city was going to get out of the decade without any real scars.

Unfortunately, that was not going to be entirely true.

Vietnam Protests, Sacks A Landmark.

In 1879, the people of Fort Collins opened the first building for their new college. It was a stately two story brick building with a large steeple on top. It served as classrooms, dormitory and administration building all in one for Colorado A and M College. Everyone was very proud of the building, which was located south of Laurel, a few hundred feet west of College Avenue.

As the years went by, the college grew and eventually built a proper administration building at the end of the Oval. This made the original building "Old Main" short for "main administration". But the building was still used a great deal for classrooms and lots of other activities. In 1899 a 900 seat auditorium was added and used for stage productions of all kinds, from then on.

The college grew, became Colorado State University in

Old Main, CSU's original building from 1879. It was used as classrooms and offices until 1970. There was also a 900 seat theater that was used for community productions. It was added on in 1899. This World War I picture was taken in 1917.

1957, and still Old Main was rolling right along with the times and continued as a classroom and office building. It was hot in the summer and cold in the winter. It was so close to the railroad tracks that whenever a train came rumbling through, which was quite often, everything in the building stopped, since you could not hear a teacher speaking. The whole building would vibrate! Nevertheless, Old Main was a much cherished landmark of both the city and the university. It was used by both, continuously.

Then came the late 1960s. Campuses all over the country were erupting in civil disobedience in protest over the war in Vietnam. In Fort Collins, the campus of CSU was much quieter than most places in the country. Certainly the rhetoric was strident. The college newspaper was filled with indignation over the war. The students were one, giant, angry sulk. However, it was still peaceful and the city and university administration considered themselves lucky.

Rumors had circulated all day on Saturday, May 8, 1970, that something dramatic was going to happen to draw atten-

Students, neighbors and bystanders all pitched in to fight the Old Main fire. The building was deliberately set fire in a Vietnam war protest in May, 1970. It was a community tragedy. (INSERT) The fire lit up the night and destroyed the building completely.

Fort Collins Library

tion to the students dissent to the Vietnam War. The campus was particularly active that day. When night fell, the campus remained active.

Then, just before 11 p.m. that Saturday night, somebody spotted smoke pouring out of the basement at Old Main. The calls flooded into the fire department.

Even before the first units of fire equipment arrived, hundreds of excited students and townspeople were on the scene, trying to put the fire out. They were literally risking their lives to save the building with hand held fire extinguishers and garden hoses. The firemen had to push the crowd out of the way to get in to fight the fire.

When they arrived the flames were climbing up the main stairway and spreading to the second floor and the steeple above. The fire was out of control. The firemen did what they could, but it was soon apparent that they were not going to be able to save the building.

The crowd grew to several thousand people and most of them were crying openly over this senseless loss for the ungainly, but distinctive building. When sun up came, all that remained was the skeleton of the smoking building. It was a complete loss.

An investigation revealed that the fire had been deliberately set in the basement of Old Main by person or persons unknown. Nobody was ever caught or accused of the crime. Old Main had become Fort Collins' casualty of the Vietnam War.

DT². Designing Tomorrow, Today.

The burning of Old Main was like a catalyst that got the people of Fort Collins moving. People in town were saying that Fort Collins was no longer the quaint little city where nothing ever happened and the big, bad world outside never invaded. Clearly, that time was over. The city was just going to have to overcome its adolescence and grow up.

The people of Fort Collins were not stupid. They could see what was happening, and they were eager to help. They reasoned that, although business was very good and the town was booming, a way was needed to meet many current needs and to plan for the future.

The answer was a citizen initiated movement to help new and old residents understand the changes that had been thrust upon them, and help in planning for the needs of the community, for today and tomorrow. They created a new organization which they called just that, "Designing Tomorrow, Today." It was nickname DT squared. It was funded partly by the city and partly by the Chamber of Commerce. The organization acted as a huge funnel to bring all of the different ideas and planning by a huge pool of interested people and organizations into a single information stream that could assist the city council in charting the path for the future and providing the most widely based plan for getting and funding city improvements.

It was a huge success, and another one of those unique times when people stepped forward and solved common problems just as they had been doing for over a hundred years. Most people did not have the slightest idea that they were repeating history, and actually didn't care. All they knew was that the needs of the city were going to be addressed.

The organization Designing Tomorrow Today, or DT² took

the extensive of ideas about city improvements from all of the various groups with an ax to grind, and got it into a city plan that could serve Fort Collins for the decades of growth that were sure to follow. It was enthusiastically endorsed by most of the groups in town. A list of specific projects were presented to the city council for review. The ideas were addressed in meetings, and were subjected to public debate. The whole process of information was spread through the media in an effort to inform as many people as possible.

Specific projects listed in the Capital Improvements program after two years of study went to the voters in February of 1973. A one cent increase in the sales tax was needed to fund the projects. 8660 people voted in the largest turn out for a city election in history until that time, and it passed overwhelmingly. From this vote came a series of civic improvements. Included in the plan was, the Lincoln Center, the new public library, the park and trail system and all sorts of general improvements to the infrastructure of the city. If you have arrived in Fort Collins since 1973, you might say that the people here then, saw you coming and made plans for your arrival.

Perhaps even more fundamental in this community project was the understanding that the process was going to have to be ongoing and continuous. Given that the city was going to continue to grow because of its attractiveness to people from all over the country, the planning would also have to continue. For the past 20 years, there have been many similar programs that have met with varying degrees of success, but the process does continue as it must.

The Big Thompson Flood.

In nearly 150 years of recorded history in Colorado and Larimer County, many tragedies and events of death and destruction have been chronicled. However, the worst of these did not happen in the distant past. Instead, it was an event that occurred in the modern era, just a generation ago. It was, by far, the worst disaster to ever come to the Poudre Valley, and, indeed, all of Colorado. It was the Big Thompson Flood in 1976.

On the afternoon of July 31, 1976, a monsoonal flow of

warm air brought large amounts of moisture up from the Gulf of Mexico. At the same time, a blast of cold polar air flowed in from the north. The two air masses collided over the Front Range of the Rocky Mountains, north of Denver and triggered several very slow moving thunderstorms.

Normally, the Big Thompson River is 25 feet wide. It spread to 250 feet at the height of the flood. At the mouth of the canyon, flood waters were estimated to be flowing at 250,000 gallons per second. Fort Collins Library

The first sprinkles of rain began to fall in Fort Collins at about 5:30 p.m. During the next hour, the rain became a traditional summer cloudburst and forced a halt in the outdoor historical pageant that was a part of the city's Bicentennial Celebration. I can remember being highly annoyed at the time, since we had worked on the pageant for weeks and had to stop right in the middle of the performance because it was raining so hard that performers and spectators alike had to run for cover.

Little did we know that another cell of that big storm was sitting, almost motionless over the mountains, west of Estes Park, and it was dropping a titanic amount of moisture on the upper watershed of the Big Thompson River. Beginning at about the same time as the rain in Fort Collins, this storm continued to drop in the same place and rained for four hours. A total of 12 inches, a whole foot of water fell over thousands of mountain acres. Nearly all of this water began to run downhill and had to go somewhere. Well, the somewhere was straight down the Big Thompson Canyon. On that Saturday night there were 3,000 people camped or staying in cabins in the canyon.

By 7 p.m., the water in the river inside the canyon began to rise rapidly. At 7:30 p.m. calls to the Larimer County Sheriff's office from area residents reported that in addition to the water rising in the river, that big rocks were falling on the highway. It was also at this time that the first warning was broadcast on radio. The warning read, "Severe thunderstorms are possible in Eastern Larimer County until 9 p.m. Local flooding can occur in low lying areas." It was a routine broadcast, but by that time some people in the Big Thompson Canyon were already fighting for their lives.

By 8 p.m. that night, rain was falling at the rate of five inches per hour with the storm at its peak.

At 8:25, State Patrolman Bill Miller radioed the first cries for help and warning to the police in Estes Park. He reported that the flooding was becoming widespread. "This is going to be awful!" he said. "Now somebody up there push the red button and get everybody within 50 miles moving, and I mean right now! We have to evacuate this canyon!"

A few minutes later, Larimer County Sheriff's Deputy, Larry Wyer told his dispatcher in Fort Collins the very same thing, but more profanely.

The Big Thompson Canyon is in Larimer County which made the Larimer County Sheriff the overall responsible agency to coordinate the actions of all the people who would be needed to react to this onrushing calamity. There was a plan to deal with a major disaster, such as a flood, in the Big Thompson Canyon, and it was rapidly put into action.

But Highway 34, going up the Big Thompson Canyon is a state road and is routinely monitored by the Colorado Highway Patrol. That night the State Troopers became the point men into the disaster area. Their job was to get into the canyon and start taking whatever emergency actions were required to preserve lives and property, lives being the main priority.

At 8:44 p.m. law enforcement agencies begin networking with one another to establish that the an emergency existed and that immediate steps were needed. The first priority was to warn everyone in the canyon and evacuate all 3,000 people before the entire canyon filled up with water and drowned everyone of them!

Down in Loveland, State Patrolman Hugh Purdy heard all the traffic on his police scanner in his home. He immediately went out and got into his patrol car and took off up the canyon. It was raining so hard that he could barely see to drive, but he was trying to go so fast that he was nearly killed at every turn he took as he drove the jagged narrows just inside the canyon. The river was a raging torrent and rose rapidly toward the road! Patrolman Purdy struggled on into the curtains of water that fell out of the black night.

At 9 p.m. Denver radio warned "that thunderstorms are moving slowly north along the Front Range and that local flooding could occur." In the Big Thompson Canyon it was raining so hard you couldn't see your hand in front of your face, and people were beginning to die.

At 9:15 p.m. Sheriff's Deputies Terry Urista and Jim Garcia radioed to the dispatcher in Fort Collins. They said that they were at Cedar Grove and that everyone should get out of the canyon and away from the river . . . NOW! The two deputies barely escaped with their lives and were trapped just above the river for two days.

At that same moment Patrolman Purdy radioed that he was in trouble. "I can't get out! I'm right in the middle of it!" Then he told the dispatcher the canyon had to be evacuated. Then his radio went dead.

Between 9:30 and 10 p.m. the harried dispatchers of all the emergency agencies stepped up their efforts to get every avail-

The only reason this house stopped floating down the river was because it hit this bridge. But the water continued its destructive path.   Fort Collins Library

able unit into the canyon and warn everyone to evacuate. A roadblock was set up at the mouth of the canyon to keep people from going in. Some people had just come to see for themselves and actually thought they could drive up the canyon and look at the big flood in the river. Others were trying to get to members of their family who were already in the canyon and for whom they were scared to death. The sheriff turned everyone away. The priority was to get everyone out. A solid line of cars where rolling out of the canyon and there was no mistaking the terror on the faces of the people as they drove by.

At 10:30 p.m. the rain began to let up. There was not a single person in the entire area that was fooled by that. The people knew that the worst was yet to come. The crest of the flood still lay many miles to the west near the top of the canyon.

Sure enough. Between 10:30 and 11 p.m., a wall of water nearly 20-feet-tall, came washing down the canyon. Billions of gallons of water, roaring in a fury beyond description, and was sweeping up cars, houses, businesses, trees, boulders and . . . people.

When the crest of the flood reached the Dam Store at the mouth of the canyon, at 11 p.m. debris began to smash into the massive supports for the enormous water siphon pipe that stretched across the road. An entire house, swept along by the flood, rammed the biggest concrete support and reduced it to gravel. The siphon collapsed onto the road. Nobody was going in or out of the canyon now. Filled with water, as it was, the pipe weighed over a million pounds.

Also at that time, the National Weather service issued its first flash flood warning of the whole night. It said, "A Flash Flood Warning is in effect until 4 a.m. for persons near the Big Thompson River from Loveland to Greeley. A Flash Flood Warning means that flooding is imminent. Take necessary precautions as required."

At that moment, the water at the mouth of the canyon was measured 19 feet above the normal level of the river. The Big Thompson would normally flow at about 165 cubic feet per second. Now the flow was over 31,000 cubic feet per second. That's 233,000 gallons of water — per second. To all of the people nearby, the flooding was a good deal more than just imminent!

Visions Along The Poudre Valley

The following morning, when the sun came up, deputies, patrolmen, mother and fathers, sons and daughters, turned back to the Big Thompson Canyon. The destruction was beyond belief. As rescue helicopters flew along the route of the canyon, the pilots reported that everything in the canyon had been laid waste. Much of the road had completely disappeared. The river had gouged new channels and changed course many times. Everywhere there was mud and debris; cars were littered by the hundreds along the canyon floor.

In the aftermath, cars and buildings were buried under many feet of mud that had been washed down by the river.

The pilots also reported that they could see many bodies buried in the mud and smashed like rag dolls. Many hundreds more were clinging to precarious safety along the slopes of the canyon, waving at the helicopters to see them and save them. The rescue operations kept the emergencies crews and helicopters busy all day long. Every person who came out had stories of terror and agony to tell. All of them repeated, many times, that they were just grateful to be alive.

The entire State of Colorado mobilized to give aid to the people of Larimer County in this most destructive natural disaster in the history of the state. Governor Dick Lamm said, "The river had reclaimed the canyon from all its intruders."

The gruesome job of recovering and identifying all the bodies went on for days. Among the first of the bodies recovered was that of State Patrolman Hugh Purdy, who was found downstream, many miles from his last known location. In the end, the death count was between 139 and 150 people. Some bodies were never recovered, and some were never identified.

When the costs were finally added up, in addition to the death toll, the river had destroyed over 600 homes and businesses and flood damage amounted to over 56 million dollars.

It took two years to rebuild the road and over ten years for the canyon to return to normal.

It was called a "thousand year flood," but that doesn't mean that it couldn't happen again tomorrow.

A Vision For You.

We have now come to the end of the narrative history of our little corner of the world covering everything from the geological roots of northern Colorado and on through each of the important periods in the history of the Poudre Valley and its principal city for over 130 years . . . Fort Collins.

This history, of course, is not complete, rather it is representative of the sense of events and people who have made the history and shaped the destiny of all Larimer County. There are many other stories to tell, and many more trails to follow. I would certainly encourage each of you, and especially if you are young, to learn more about our history on your own. Believe me, all of the materials that I use are readily and easily available at the Public Library.

Once a person asked me what *I* got out of all this study of our history.

"Me? — Illumination."

I have learned that there aren't very many new things in this world, at least as far as people are concerned. There is substantially no difference in a father's desire to have the best he can for his family, today than there was 150 years ago. The quality of the human spirit is unchanged throughout all of the struggles, strife and momentous changes that have been thrust upon us over the period of a mere eight generations.

As I write this passage, the population of Fort Collins is 100,000 people. That is ten times the population of just over 40 years ago. Does that mean that 40 years from now that northern Colorado will have a population of a million people?

The founders of Fort Collins, Joe Mason, Bill Stover, Franklin Avery, B.F. Hottel, Auntie Stone and all the rest would be shocked senseless if they could see what has become of their brave little town, along a mostly quiet little river, for which they had so many dreams.

Without a doubt, they would want to know, if they could ask you directly, how you like the way its turning out? Very likely you would have volumes to tell them, good and bad, about just what you think about Fort Collins and its future.

Then, these venerable founders would say, "Why are you telling me all this? Our time is over. We did the best we could with what we had. You are going to have to do the same. We planned for lifetimes beyond ours and so will you. When it seemed like we couldn't get anybody to agree about anything, we got together and found a way, and so will you."

So, in the way that Americans have of acting out their dreams, the people of Fort Collins of yesterday and today, believe that anything is possible out here on the wild frontier. You abandoned the word impossible when you came here from somewhere else.

The future shines with certain promise.

For me, its enough to say that all of this is "So Dear to My Heart . . . these Visions Along the Poudre Valley."

Modern Fort Collins. In 1995, the city had grown to over 55 square miles and had a population of 100,000 people. Paul Nielsen